LIVING BUILDING MAKERS:
Creating Sustainable Buildings That Renew Our World

An Ecotone Publishing Book 2019

ECOTONE PUBLISHING – AN IMPRINT OF THE INTERNATIONAL LIVING FUTURE INSTITUTE

For more information write:

Ecotone Publishing
1501 East Madison Street, Suite 150
Seattle, WA 98122
ecotone@living-future.org

AUTHOR: Jonathan A. Wright
EDITOR: Mary Adam Thomas
BOOK DESIGN: Johanna Björk / softfirm
COVER PHOTOGRAPHS: Bill Kern

LIBRARY OF CONGRESS CONTROL NUMBER: 2019934401

Library of Congress Cataloging-in Publication Data
ISBN: 978-0-9972368-6-6

1. ARCHITECTURE   2. ENVIRONMENT

First Edition

Printed in Canada on FSC-certified paper, processed Chlorine-Free, using vegetable-based ink.

CONTENTS

> "If we want to
> make things better,
> we have to make
> better things."
>
> JONATHAN A. WRIGHT

4

Living Building MakersLiving Building Makers

DEDICATION

For the skill, spirit, determination, and humor of the whole Wright Builders staff, past and present, who are the heart and soul of this effort, I am most grateful. You endured the uncertainty and the pressure, found and maintained the path forward, and accomplished all the work with courage and wisdom. You led all the makers, especially me, on this journey. In your hands, all our hands, the future lives and thrives.

For my wife, Meg Kelsey Wright, who has shared the excitement of the project from its inception. As a professional musician, and an excellent writer herself, she was again, as with my earlier books, a dedicated, fastidious, and generous reader for scope and detail. Her musical ear found new resonances for the words, helping them into sentences, always working to shed extraneous notes. All along the way Meg was at hand and willing. As a legendary teacher, she has appreciated my own progress as a teacher and storyteller. The book has brought us new understandings, love, and appreciation of each other and the planet. Thank you. This is your book too, sweetheart.

6

Acknowledgements:
A TIME FOR GRATITUDE

Like a broad lake over an abundant aquifer, this book, and the Living Building Challenge it celebrates, has many fresh and prolific sources. The people who have made the Challenge, these two projects, and this book possible are many, diverse, and wonderful. Here I continue the "thank you note" that is really at the core of *Living Building Makers*.

My first exposure to the Living Building Challenge came from Amherst architect Bruce Coldham who voluntarily undertook to bring the Smith College Bechtel Environmental Center through to Living Building certification. Along the way, Wright Builders, Inc. provided pre-construction planning and pricing to Bruce's team, and we got our first look at the Challenge. Roger Cooney, vice president of design and estimating at Wright Builders, was really excited by this exposure and helped us all connect with what was at first a bewildering process. He introduced us to Charley Stevenson of Integrated Eco Strategy, who kept us engaged and encouraged all through the process.

On our first trip to Seattle, in December 2013, we were welcomed to the Bullitt Center by Denis Hayes of the Bullitt Foundation and the entire design and construction team that had produced an extraordinary building and Living Building Challenge milestone. When I asked, "Where do we start on materials?" the answer, almost instantly, was "weather-stripping." There were chuckles and murmurs all around the sixth floor conference table. But if you imagine what it takes to avoid neoprene and PVC, and have a tight building, with lots of foot traffic, this was wildly good advice. For that, and the full kit of support, thank you to that entire team.

My first visit to an International Living Future Institute (ILFI) unConference included a stop at a book launch and signing by Jason F. McLennan, whose fingerprints are all over the Challenge (which makes sense, since he conceived it). I told him that each of the seven performance area Petals reflected all the things that I had at one time or another wanted to do in my building career, but they were just too big, daunting, and shapeless to undertake alone. Now there was a way to think and advance! We shared a hug, which I felt wrapped around us all through the making of these buildings. Thanks, Jason.

Amanda Sturgeon, CEO at the International Living Future Institute, asked me to tea when she was in Boston in the spring of 2017. I had struggled to conceptualize how this book would come to be. Amanda said quietly, before the tea had even steeped, "Jonathan, every time I see you, you tell me a story and I repeat those stories over and over again. So maybe just write down those stories. People want to hear them." That's how this book came to be. Simple, maybe, but insight, intelligence, and support are at the heart of great leadership. Thank you, Amanda, for that and everything else.

At each and every turn, the Institute has been forthcoming, energetic, upbeat, and helpful. To the ILFI staff: My hope is that some of these stories will startle you into realizing anew what an extraordinary thing it is that you do. You are wonderful.

To the teams that created the sixteen certified Living Buildings that came before ours, congratulations, and thanks for creating the bow wave. We needed the lift!

I have dedicated this book in part to the Wright Builders team, bearing a heart full of gratitude. Without the team's curiosity and stamina, along with their openness, knowledge, and intelligence, the projects would not have succeeded. In these stories, you will meet the makers of the R.W. Kern Center and the Hitchcock Center for the Environment. To each maker, I say thank you for your work and your story.

Mark Ledwell, now president of Wright Builders, always reminded me that I was responsible for mixing what he called the LBK — the Living Building Kool-Aid — that was sipped and toasted throughout these projects. The recipe is still classified but the legend lives. Mark managed the Hitchcock Center expertly, with his uniquely upbeat problem-solving skills and encyclopedic construction knowledge. Foreman Jim Small also provided a steady hand, expert layout, and his own low-key friendly enthusiasm and leadership.

At the R.W. Kern Center, the combination of Project Manager Tom Lucia and John Averill, foreman, was the other dream team, always ready with options for developing nuances, and never fazed. Both teams were backed up by Linda Gaudreau, Andrew Solem, Ann Ledwell, Scott Belanger, and many others. Without fail, these people set the ambitions of the project into motion every day, taking the inspiration in and generating their own unique leadership.

A particular thank you to Wright Builders' Melissa Caldwell for leaning into planning and organizing the reunions, collecting and uploading images, and a genuine level of enthusiasm for the book project as part of her commitment to a healing and regenerative future.

Carl Weber was the rock in building the R.W. Kern Center. He managed the money, gave us heart, offered friendship and encouragement, and delivered details, decisions, and humor.

Whether hunched over his dining table with me trying to make sense of contract language in this world of Living Buildings, or guiding us through a maze of decisions, Chris Riddle brought his lifetime of architecture and Amherst town experience to the Hitchcock Center, for which I am very grateful.

John Robinson helped Carl Weber at the R.W. Kern Center and Chris Riddle at the Hitchcock Center with a long list of owner project management chores. Larry Archey and Mark Spiro were both on board early in the R.W. Kern Center project, providing crucial leadership and giving us confidence and support.

Gaye Hill, the Hampshire College Board of Trustees chair, was a bulwark of support, enthusiasm, and stunning generosity, leading the whole Board to embrace these ambitions. Jonathan Lash, as president of Hampshire College, entrusted us with this emblem of the College's mission, nature, and future, unlike any assignment or opportunity, ever, for me or anyone else involved. I think he, too, became captivated by what was in the making and delighted in celebrating it.

Hampshire faculty, especially those who appear in the book, saw the opportunity for innovative teaching and curriculum, and took the R.W. Kern Center to new heights as a tool and as a guide. They provided me with endless inspiration.

The Hitchcock Board of Directors and Building Committee walked the long walk from concept to idea to funding and reality, with guidance from Julie Johnson. Julie's 100 percent day-and-night commitment to the Living Building Challenge, and her inclusion of Wright Builders in the planning process, was an honor to share. All through the Hitchcock Center, the staff, educators, and administrators, and volunteers have utilized the building in ways that compound the pride of the makers. Thank you.

The entire team appreciates the support and responsiveness of the Town of Amherst and its Select Board members at every step. The late and beloved Amherst Town Manager John Musante was full on with us from the start. And David Ziomek, as acting town manager, carried on guiding the regulatory processes with thoroughness and commitment. The inspection processes were collaborative and very professional. It was an honor to have oversight from people who know the work so well.

Jason Jewhurst and Jason Forney of Bruner/Cott Architects taught us well and shared so much about how beauty is made in the long journey from pencil sketch to mortared stone. We still retain a special affection and connection. Christopher Nielsen mastered the details and guided us at each step as the collection of materials became animated in our hands. I think he likes what we made for him!

Sara Draper handled mountains of detailed correspondence and collaborated with the construction team on all the materials vetting and record keeping. Later, she assembled the documentation for certification. That made her career shift — to director of communication and outreach at the R.W. Kern Center — a natural. A friend, collaborator, masterful convener, and rock star!

Sam Batchelor of designLAB architects designed a building so worth the extra and remarkable effort, and so reflective of the mission and feel of the Hitchcock Center. Kelly Ard Haigh crushed the drawings and detailing with a complete design drawing set like we seldom see. They understood the Hitchcock Center at a metabolic level, which is amazing to observe and to share.

One afternoon, I sat in a chair in my writing study and read Bill Kern an early draft of a chapter from a book I later decided not to write. He listened, then leaned forward on the couch and said, "I think the story begins in the third sentence of the second paragraph." "How do you know?" I asked, startled. "Well, that's where the hook is and that's how you read it." Bill's keen interest, insight, and thirst for details of people and story are part of the inspiration for this book. His support of the R.W. Kern Center, the ILFI, and this book project mean the world to me. Bill brought a film maker's eye and expertise to the effort. It's because of Bill that I could write this book and find its meaning in my own time. I am changed and forever grateful.

Lee Kern, Ralph Kern's widow, always provided a cheerful and wise presence, gracious and enthused. Everything that the R.W. Kern Center touches, touches her back. We can see her when we look in the mirror, and we are so grateful.

Ecotone Publishing's Editor-in-Chief Michael Berrisford devoted himself to coaching and supporting me in this effort at every level. He has taught me how to engage and discern in ways that I could not have imagined. Michael selected Mary Adam Thomas, a considerable author in her own right, to be the editor, and Mary trained me in every detail. Mary not only wore the hat of editor, she carried the tools of a writer, co-conspirator, spiritual advisor, revisionist, cat herder, and extraordinary English language expert. This book is packed with the fruits of Michael and Mary's caring and insight. Michael also selected designer Johanna Björk for this next in her series of designs for Ecotone, and what a superb eye, design sense, humor, and energy she brought to this collaboration. It's sunny where you are. Thank you!

Foreword

BY JONATHAN LASH

A big red barn figures in this tale. A dairy barn belonging to one of the several family farms quietly purchased in the late 1960s to create Hampshire College's 843 acre campus. The "Red Barn" and the neighboring farmhouse became Hampshire's Admissions Center, a meeting place, and one of the best wedding venues in Western Massachusetts. Generations of students entered through that portal which looks across rolling meadows to the north face of the Holyoke Range. Glorious.

When the college opened in the fall of 1970, however, the Red Barn was an empty cow barn. The following year a crew of students, faculty, and staff went to work rebuilding it. Hands-on learning. Students clambered up hand-hewn beams to insulate the roof, swung hammers to tear out rotted stalls, and sanded the hoof-worn floors. Then they met to argue about curriculum. Everyone felt that they were building a college and creating a new inquiry and experience-based approach to education. Building their own education, students came to believe that they could learn anything and solve any problem.

Jonathan Wright was a member of that first entering class, and by the end of his final year he and a friend had founded a little construction company to tide them over while they decided what to do. Fifty years later he has a reputation as a skilled craftsman, a successful and generous businessman, and the Pioneer Valley's leading green builder.

I met Jonathan shortly after I became Hampshire College's sixth president. He came to the Red Barn to read from a book of poetry he had just published. He was accompanied by a friend playing a haunting shakuhachi flute. It was magical. "So this, I thought, is what a builder who went to Hampshire does." Jonathan and I talked about the school he loved, its combination of old farm houses and 1970s brutalist architecture built on the assumption that electricity would come from nuclear plants and would be "too cheap to meter." Electrically heated. Uninsulated. Even some single-paned glass. All wrong.

We could do so much better.

This book is, in large part, the story of the fulfillment of that ambition, and how the resulting structure, the R.W. Kern Center, became Jonathan Wright's masterpiece.

At about the same time I met Jonathan, I saw a story in The New York Times about the Bullitt Foundation's decision to build a "Living Building," a zero waste, net zero energy urban office building that added to rather than diminished beauty and social justice. I contacted Denis Hayes, the president of the Foundation and an old friend to congratulate him. "Maybe," he responded, "Hampshire will build one?" It was a timely question. The Red Barn had disadvantages as an admissions center. Half a mile from classrooms and student housing, visiting families spent half of an hour-long tour walking up the hill to the main campus and back down again, following student tour guides walking backwards and talking about inquiry-driven education. The barn was a part of that when that first class entered, but that was history. Now visitors saw nothing of what the school did or stood for as they arrived, got their orientation, and formed first impressions of the community.

Could a building express our values, focus the campus, and not just house, but be part of our educational mission? Could a building speak and teach, engaging visitors and community members alike?

On a cold, bright March afternoon four years later, Jonathan hosted a picnic lunch in the newly closed-in atrium of the R.W. Kern Center. He had invited the crew and managers from Wright Builders and all of the sub-contractors who had worked on the building. It was a "thank you," and a chance to acknowledge that they had participated in something unique, and each, caught up in the spirit of the project, had done extraordinary work: plumbers, electricians, stone masons, carpenters, glaziers, and heating contractors, who'd worked with systems and specifications they had never seen before. Jonathan spoke about the challenges the project had presented, and his gratitude to each of them for helping to meet those challenges. Jonathan and I, and Bill Kern, the Hampshire alum whose family became major donors to the building in order to name it in honor of his father, spoke about why the building meant so much. Buildings are the source of 40 percent of U.S. carbon emissions, places where we spend most of our time and thus do much to determine the quality of our lives and health and interactions with one another. Here was a building whose challenge was to address all of that — full of light and locally sourced natural materials — the warmth of wood, the wisdom of stone, century-old planks recovered from an abandoned mill in what was once an industrial center on the fast streams of Western Massachusetts; a warm, transparent place where all the paths through the campus crossed.

Jonathan invited his guests to speak about their experience as they ate their pizza and salad. One after another they told stories of parents who had worked in the construction trades and died young from exposure to toxic materials in solvents, adhesives, paints, and finishes. "This building is a whole different story. I stay in here for lunch, other buildings I get out when I can. I feel like my kids might be able to follow me and live a healthy life." They expressed pride, wonder, and hope. They did their best work. The building was doing its job.

Within a few months, before the building had opened, a group of students working with their first-year tutorial professors — a biologist, a hydrologist, and a mathematician — constructed laboratory and mathematical models of the building's plant-based wastewater treatment system. The building uses advanced composting toilets, so the wastewater is from hand washing, drinking fountains, and the espresso machine in the Kern Kafé. About 5 percent of the water a normal building of this size would use, all collected from rainwater harvested on-site. The waste is filtered through indoor plants, and then fed to a managed wetland just outside the building. The system drew wide interest, and the students' work was published in a scientific journal, with their names listed alongside their

professors' names. It won them a grant, which took them to an international environmental engineering conference, where they won a competition against graduate students for design of wastewater systems. So, the building was teaching.

In its 17,800 square feet, the R.W. Kern Center contains Hampshire College's admissions and financial aid operations, glass-walled classrooms, exhibit space, and a light-filled, caffeinated social space where people meet, students study, and visiting families encounter the school. Student docents, admissions guides, and Kern Kafé baristas alike handle visitors' questions about how the building works, and the implications of the operating data reported on a big flat-screen dashboard. Families are encouraged to try to solve the ten puzzles developed by a game design professor and built into the structure, each with a message about the building.

Wright Builders actually built two buildings on the Hampshire campus during this period. The Hitchcock Center for the Environment created a new headquarters and education center near the Hampshire Farm, and it too is a "Living Building," though it solves the challenges of net positive impact in different ways than the R.W. Kern Center. Every "Living Building" pushes the boundaries of materials and design, and also the skills — and sometimes the patience — of those who build them. Jonathan has become the master of this process, and many of us urged him to write a book about it. He agreed. I anticipated something fairly technical — a guide for the perplexed — not the extraordinary prose-poem that emerged a year later and became this book. It is a story of what is possible, and what striving to achieve what is possible does for all of the people involved.

Commentary

BY JULIE JOHNSON

"Would you do it again?" was the question asked of me upon entering the hotel lobby for my first Living Future unConference in Seattle in 2017. To my surprise, I found myself wholly unprepared to answer the question.

We were all there for the conference and we made shorthand introductions. I introduced myself as the executive director of the Hitchcock Center for the Environment in Amherst, Massachusetts. We had just opened our new environmental learning center, designed and built to meet the Living Building Challenge. I was there to deliver a presentation on how we were using our building as an innovative teaching tool to promote environmental literacy.

None of my lobby companions had yet been involved in a Living Building project, but they knew the Challenge pushed significant limits. Hence their question: "So knowing what you know now, would you do another Living Building Challenge project?"

The question was intended for a quick, definitive answer — yes or no. But for whatever reason, at that moment, I could not formulate a declarative statement. I walked away perplexed. What stopped me from simply saying "Yes!"? I had answered different versions of this very same question every day for the last eight years. I had persuaded my Board of Directors, as fiduciary overseers, to take on the cost premium of a Living Building Challenge project knowing the added value it would create for our Center. I had "sold" the Living Building Challenge to donors, funders, and contributors to secure the millions of dollars needed to successfully complete this project. And I had also facilitated countless hours of conversation with staff on how the Living Building Challenge would profoundly benefit our work as environmental educators.

Pursuing the Challenge is not only core to the Hitchcock Center's mission, it is core to pioneering a new pathway to human survivability. We are living among 7.4 billion people and counting. Human-caused climate change is threatening our very existence. With every major ecological system in rapid decline, it doesn't take much to know that business as usual is no longer a viable option.

So when it became clear that the Hitchcock Center's previous building and site could not support the growth we needed, we knew we had to look to the outer limits of possibilities in creating the most environmentally sustainable building possible.

At the time, there were many green building certifications, rating systems, and labels to choose from including the most popular — LEED. All provided solid, well-reasoned pathways toward environmental sustainability, but after much research we found none as visionary as the Living Building Challenge. Its definition of sustainability is vastly different from any of the others. It goes well beyond addressing the environmental impacts of the built environment through net zero energy, water, and waste mandates. It also requires projects to vigorously address issues of social justice, equity, beauty, advocacy, and so much more.

As environmental educators working in the field for over a combined 200+ years, we all agreed that the Challenge spoke to us. The bedrock of environmental education in the 21st century is to equip people with the knowledge, understanding, skills, and motivation to restore the health of the natural systems upon which all life depends, while also creating an economically prosperous and socially just future for all.

The Living Building Challenge is not about constructing a building; it's about constructing a movement. It brings people together from disparate professions, perspectives, and places in a process of learning, pushing boundaries, facing fears, discovering commonalities, and finding solutions to some of the most complex environmental challenges facing society today.

For all of these reasons, there was nothing that should have prevented me from answering that early morning question with an unequivocal "Yes!"

Arriving at the opening ceremony, I was ready to let go of the question and just be a passive participant at the conference. Not only was I jet-lagged, it occurred to me that I might also have a minor case of executive director burnout. All I wanted to do was sit down and "check-out." But to my chagrin, I was immediately asked to stand up. Oh please don't ask me to introduce myself to the person next to me. I had already failed miserably in the hotel lobby.

To my delight, we were led through a beautiful series of Tai Chi exercises by the most elegant and mesmerizing woman I had ever seen. I had never attempted Tai Chi and it was clear that nearly all of the conference attendees had not either. Over 1,000 of us spent our first ten minutes together breathing deeply, holding poses, and focusing inward as this small woman with the soothing voice expertly led us in an activity that immediately made me feel connected and alive.

That was when I realized this conference was going to be different. Over the course of the next several days, I was deeply moved by the courage, creativity and passion of the people I met and heard. They were a mix of artists, civil rights leaders, journalists, designers, builders, engineers, educators, policymakers, and youth leaders; you name it, they were there.

The conference reconnected me to the origins of the Hitchcock Center's Living Building Challenge project — to serve as a change agent. We chose the Living Building Challenge not as a means to an end, to create a new building, but as

a commitment to making change for a better world. I now understand why I couldn't answer the question posed to me that first day. The question implied that the project was over when actually its living legacy had just begun!

The Living Building Challenge is not about constructing a building; it's about constructing a movement. It brings people together from disparate professions, perspectives, and places in a process of learning, pushing boundaries, facing fears, discovering commonalities, and finding solutions to some of the most complex environmental challenges facing society today.

The following stories are about the makers who helped create two remarkable Living Buildings in one small town, highlighting the way the process has forever changed them.

Author Jonathan Wright tells these stories with eloquence and wit through the unique lens of construction manager to both projects. Jonathan is a Renaissance man who lives life through his hands, heart, and mind. He is a teacher, a builder, a philosopher, a poet, and an activist.

Living Building Makers is a work of passion for Jonathan and I am truly grateful for its uplifting message. It has given me a new perspective on my own personal and professional work as an environmental educator and leader. It should be read by anyone who is looking for inspiration in their own journey to create a better world.

Introduction

Every day for several years, women and men carried out seemingly ordinary work-related tasks to accomplish something extraordinary. In weather ranging from below zero to nearly 100 degrees Fahrenheit, in thunderstorms and ice, amid crisp fall winds and soggy summer humidity, indoors and outdoors, they joined hands with others who dreamed, planned, strategized, and focused intently on countless details. Along the way, they were assisted by everything from massive cranes and power tools to shovels and hand-held computers. They were architects, engineers, painters, plumbers, timber framers, craftspeople, skilled operators, project managers, college leaders, and educators. Together, they became Living Building makers.

The term "makers" casts a net that includes people of all ages, cultures, native languages, and backgrounds. Individuals and collaborators, professionals and amateurs, inventors and innovators are all connected by creativity and a passion to transform concepts into real things. Over time, they have painted on cave walls and canvases, shaped stones and timber, fitted pipe and glass, and repurposed earth-sourced materials of all kinds to create new and beautiful things. Makers transform ideas from their minds through their hearts to their hands.

Wielding planks and stones, fasteners and fittings, focus and humor, makers constructed their individual and collective legacies on an otherwise quiet college campus in New England between 2012 and 2016. This book tells some of the stories of how creating Living Buildings changed these makers'

view of their vocations. The stories show how this dedicated group of professionals transformed a small yet significant corner of the world by the way they leaned into their work.

....

Two remarkable pieces of design and construction came to life not quite simultaneously on the bucolic campus of Hampshire College in Amherst, Massachusetts as an unusual set of twins. The parent organizations were in their forties and fifties. The structures were not coached by the same midwives. The smaller one, the Hitchcock Center for the Environment, was conceived earlier and born later in a gestational nuance, while the R.W. Kern Center was on a different developmental schedule and came to life earlier, larger, and more quickly.

How was the creation of world-class Living Buildings achieved in the context of these two modestly funded organizations? It was a confluence of bold vision, leadership, determination, skill, hope, and generosity. The joining of these arterial vessels of energy revealed itself to be a mighty stream. What the projects had in common was a powerful sense of place in a welcoming town and region devoted to education and sustainability. They shared a builder, Wright Builders, Inc., of Northampton, Massachusetts, a company I founded in 1974. They shared a beautiful rural campus and continue to share the compelling mission and ethos of the International Living Future Institute, whose Living Building Challenge asks, "What does good look like?"

How can the making and remaking of the built environment that we all inhabit and depend on reach beyond mitigating the damage humans have caused and actually contribute to the resilience, restoration, and healing of our troubled Earth?

Equally important is the question of how the people who take part in the Living Building Challenge's great forward motion are changed, moved, and healed. It is these people, the makers, who do the daily moving.

I am one of the makers — a convener of teams, champion of good works, worrier, and celebrant, whose personal and professional life was forever altered by my connection to these projects through the Living Building Challenge. I have a multi-tiered relationship with the Hitchcock Center and R.W. Kern Center projects because my company, Wright Builders, built both structures. The roots go deeper yet, as I am an alumnus of Hampshire College's first entering class and I have lived in Hampshire County for nearly fifty years. I have had the great honor of working for decades with many of the makers celebrated in this book. Nothing inspires and humbles me more than great craft transformed into art — everyday work passionately expressed and completed efficiently.

The question and mystery of how talent and skill are paired with purposeful passion, and deployed to make beautiful and functional things, has intrigued me my whole life. The roots go back generations and come alive in my childhood exposure to unique craftsmen, characters, and professionals. I grew up in a house full of scholars and college teachers, with lots of big thoughts, interesting ideas, and captivating stories spun around the dinner table from experiences all over the world. My mother was a pioneer in a male-dominated academic world, changing the way modern China would be studied henceforth. My father had a knack for getting nineteen-year-olds onto the edges of their seats early in the morning in lectures about eighth-century China. He taught me that a professional is "someone seized by their subject."

In summers around Long Island Sound, I messed around in sailboats. I inhaled more than my share of lead and copper dust and fumes in backyards and boatyards, in preparation for time on the water. I can still taste the sweetness of that paint sanding dust from past projects. I was drawn to a neglected basement workbench to cut, pound, bend, and fasten anything that was around, making my first bentwood furniture with an odd plank of mahogany and hand tools at age fourteen. I was beginning a journey of discovery where ideas were captivating, but making things was magical.

My search for the college that would best suit my interests and hold my attention ended when I found Hampshire and joined

The term "makers" casts a net that includes people of all ages, cultures, native languages, and backgrounds. Individuals and collaborators, professionals and amateurs, inventors and innovators are all connected by creativity and a passion to transform concepts into real things.

its pioneering first-year class in 1970. Considered then and now to be an "experimenting college," Hampshire provided me with a non-traditional educational environment committed to integrated and cross-disciplinary learning, where I could explore, write, question, and converse in its unconventional setting. I have always learned from and been inspired by the eclectic people around me: fellow students, teachers, writers, tradespeople, family members, and coworkers. At Hampshire College, I had access to an extraordinary group, which put me at the helm of my own education, and allowed me to pursue what interested me most by exploring different "modes of inquiry."

After graduating in 1974 and deferring a writing career for a few years (which turned into decades), my focus began shifting closer to a recognition and celebration of the beauty and peril in the natural world. My developing work in design and construction began probing into early ideas of solar energy and sustainable building. All these years later, my interests now center on how the goal of a sustainable, renewable, life-centered built environment can help confront and reverse, with increased urgency, the threats of climate change and destruction. How can a small business help create a work milieu of innovation, craftsmanship, friendship, humor, and excellence? Attributes gleaned from home to Hampshire, and reflected in organizations, furniture, buildings, and friendships, mark my waypoints along the journey to becoming a maker.

In re-inventing myself over time from student to poet to passable carpenter, into business person, better-than-novice finance guy, marketing novitiate, designer, developer, and then back to writer, I come back again and again to admire and appreciate those around me, all of whom know more about their work than I do. You will meet some of them in the pages that follow.

....

A sea change came to Hampshire College in 2011 with the arrival of President Jonathan Lash. He came from the World Resources Institute, which he self-described as a "do-tank" rather than a think tank, and immediately saw the opportunity for Hampshire to ignite its mission through a focus on sustainability. The College motto — "To Know is Not Enough" — resonates throughout the world of all work. Jonathan Lash understood that we have to act if we want change. We have to make things, and make better things, if we want to make things better.

When Hampshire College sought pre-construction advice regarding a new building that aspired to the Living Building Challenge, my firm came quickly to the fore. Our job as a locally-grown company with regional knowledge and experience was to help find the materials that were close at hand but perhaps hiding in plain view. We undertook to find ways to identify and inspire a team of would-be makers to create the R.W. Kern Center. We participated in the very early planning of the project, including interviewing architecture firms. How lucky we were that architects Jason Jewhurst and Jason Fourney from Bruner/Cott Architects were selected! Wright Builders was also integrated into the early meetings and goal-setting exercises for the larger campus community. Together, we embraced the challenge of building something extraordinary from the beginning, joined in our common purpose. We

never knew the full weight of what we all carried until Living Building certification was achieved in 2018, and the load lifted as if by balloon. Elation, disbelief, and exultation swirled.

About six months into the R.W. Kern Center planning, the private non-profit Hitchcock Center for the Environment was advancing its planning for a new net zero educational facility sited at the edge of the Hampshire College campus. They needed some advice from the project already underway across the campus and Larry Archey, director of facilities at Hampshire at that time, was also on the Hitchcock Center building committee. The concept plans were complete, but they were seeking a reality check on cost and needed some local knowledge about materials suitable for meeting the Living Building Challenge. Larry encouraged them to seek us out. Think of it this way: even the best captains need harbor pilots, so that's where Wright Builders came in. We helped the Hitchcock Center and designLAB architects figure out how to construct a remarkable building within the financial parameters they could afford.

While both institutions aspired to create innovative buildings that operated as elegantly as nature's architecture, neither of these projects had lavish budgets. The risks that accompanied such lofty goals were also great, as there was virtually no template or model to follow. The path toward achievement depended on the collaboration of individuals and teams, meeting in a common space and place to search and discover. That ethos spread to everyone on the teams because it is in our human nature to pursue adventure. Such spirit and kinship may be pushed down in some organizations by endless toil, but I believe it is part of our physical and spiritual makeup.

The voices and words captured in the pages that follow are not the ones we usually read in books and magazines about design and architecture. Here, we begin our acquaintance with people whose lifework is often lost or hidden, misunderstood, and under-valued. Most of it is buried in the gypsum-board coffins that many institutional and public buildings have become.

One step deeper, we find that the Living Building Challenge focuses not just on the toxicity of the final product and caring for the end users, but delves into all of the materials and environmental effects of manufacturing and delivery, tracking these back to the ocean, forest, or mine. The Challenge distinguishes itself further by going beyond performance and materials. It values social equity as well as celebrating beauty and culture, focusing on what's best for the planet and its people. This care for the workers, their colleagues, and their families is embedded in the Living Building Challenge, providing a deep affirmation and meaning for working men and women that cannot be over-stated. Lives of people we know and love are saved by working without toxins.

Living Building Makers is my curated collection of stories celebrating the people who, through their craft and skill, shared the common purpose of bringing the built environment to life for the benefit of all humans and our shared environment. Each chapter captures some of the insights, creativity, and discoveries of the often-unsung individuals. Builders, tradespeople, designers, engineers, educators, supporters, craftspeople, and owners all rolled up their sleeves and unrolled the plans. They all played a part in creating two of the greenest buildings in the world that happen, hardly by accident, to stand on the campus of Massachusetts' renowned Hampshire College.

When you journey through these stories and, I hope, visit these buildings, stay awhile. Pause and let the energy of their abundant life lift you. You, too, are a maker and your experience in and around these remarkable structures will give you your own story to tell.

JONATHAN A. WRIGHT, 2019

from TO BE OF USE

The work of the world
is common as mud.

Botched, it smears the hands,
crumbles to dust.

But the thing worth doing
well done

has a shape that satisfies,
clean and evident.

Greek amphoras for wine or oil,

Hopi vases that held corn,
are put in museums

but you know they were
made to be used.

The pitcher cries for water to carry
and a person for work that is real.

MARGE PIERCY

What Else Did You Draw?

AFTER REVIEWING THE PERFECTLY PROFESSIONAL BUT NOT YET AWE-INSPIRING PROPOSED BUILDING DRAWINGS FOR THE R.W. KERN CENTER, Hampshire College President Jonathan Lash looked up and asked, "What else did you draw? What other ideas did you have that you haven't shown us?"

That late morning in Cambridge, in the early summer of 2013, a group representing the College crowded around the conference table at the office of Bruner/Cott Architects. Finishing the last of the sandwiches, pickles, and chips and not quite yet into the cookies, we were looking at the drawings Bruner/Cott had submitted for Hampshire's new signature building. The sketches were certainly serviceable, but they weren't yet striking the dramatic chord we were looking for.

Prompted by President Lash's question, architects Jason Jewhurst and Jason Forney simultaneously sprung up out of their chairs, but then hesitated almost in mid-air as a senior partner weighed in. "We'll send you some PDFs this afternoon." Lash looked over at me and then back at the two Jasons (as they later became known) and said, "Well, how about right now?" The young architects tore out of the room and came back grinning, both carrying armloads of yellow tracing paper covered with the sketches they had stashed under their desks. These were covered with penciled ideas that had been previously set aside in favor of the more practical plan they had presented to the College.

As we leafed through the new pile, we began to see elements of the best design ideas that had been submitted by all of the various other design teams. It was all there — the curves, the angles, the dynamic forms. Suddenly the room filled with comments and exclamations as the array of creativity and ingenuity was

Creating Sustainable Buildings That Renew Our World

Bruner/Cott
team and College
representatives mine
the treasure trove of
discarded sketches.

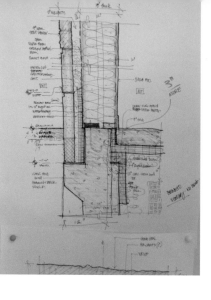

LEFT:
Big picture
planning session at
Hampshire College.

RIGHT:
Wall details for the
R.W. Kern Center
begin to take shape.

"Every time I or someone else would propose something practical and predictable, the community would go flat and lifeless. When something really outrageous, brilliant, and innovative came forward, the energy on campus would soar."

JONATHAN LASH, HAMPSHIRE COLLEGE PRESIDENT

All that creative design inhabiting and thriving around Boston and Cambridge helped us recognize the design team's capacities, potential, and talents. Jewhurst said to me, "It's a crazy process in our profession that we have to pick one submission to send to the client and then just hope for the best." I thought to myself, "Almost as brutal as being a contractor!"

In that tumble of almost-discarded tracing paper the two architects had keyed in to Hampshire's unique mission. They could turn the best of all their ideas into a fresh and stunning concept. The cores of their lifelong career commitments to sustainability started to take on new form that morning, and would continue to take shape as they engaged with the College's values and with the Living Building Challenge. The fire was lit.

spread out and recognized. Bruner/Cott had it all in the raw in their office, but had chosen to present a simple, practical, less adventurous plan to accommodate the College's modest means and budget.

It is unusual for a construction manager to be included on an institutional project team before the architects are selected, so this was a rare view into the workings of designer selection. The day had begun with a tour of a re-purposed power plant at Harvard University that Bruner/Cott had converted to workspace for the engineering staff. We moved on to the Yawkey Center for Student Services at Boston University, which included meeting rooms, a counseling center, hang-out space and more than thirty separate food preparation stations capable of serving literally thousands of diners on three levels.

When I asked Lash about his early months at Hampshire, he said, "Every time I or someone else would propose something practical and predictable, the community would go flat and lifeless. When something really outrageous, brilliant, and innovative came forward, the energy on campus would soar." So it was for those of us that morning in Cambridge, when the R.W. Kern Center seemed to suddenly rise up and stand on its own two feet.

Tour de Force

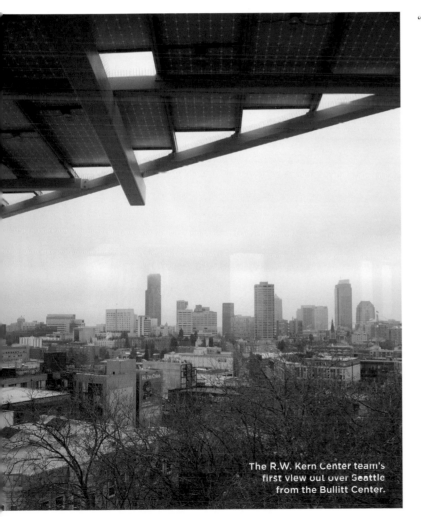

The R.W. Kern Center team's first view out over Seattle from the Bullitt Center.

"IT HAD TO GO WELL OR I MIGHT HAVE BEEN OUT OF A JOB," MUSED CARL WEBER. HE WAS NEW AS A PROJECT MANAGER AT Hampshire College when he arranged for the whole R.W. Kern Center team to travel to Seattle in December 2013 to tour the newly completed Bullitt Center and meet with the Bullitt Foundation and International Living Future Institute teams. At 52,000 square feet, the six-story Bullitt Center more than raised the bar for what was possible in the Living built environment. We wanted to learn all we could by visiting these visionary people in their stunning building, which we came to call the "mother ship."

A cold snap had barged into Seattle hours ahead of us, freezing the outdoor fountains at our hotel and adding a cold wind to the winter grey at forty-seven degrees north. When we reached the Bullitt Center, we gathered in its western-facing street-level offices, not quite yet fully furnished, and I noticed immediately that no artificial lighting was needed. How exactly had warmth and serenity replaced chilly grey in a space of concrete and glass on this midwinter day?

Members of the Bullitt Center team began our tour by showing us a wall-high banner of hundreds of different compounds of Red List chemicals named in the Living Building Challenge Materials Petal as off limits because of their toxicity. The items listed on the banner had been reviewed but rejected for the Bullitt Center project (many of them had been misspelled by the manufacturers, thus leading to even more blind alleys of research for the Bullitt

Seattle's Bullitt Center with its solar array permitted as an "awning" takes its graceful place on a busy street corner, as its irresistible staircase rises on the left.

TOP:
Inside the Bullitt Center.

LEFT:
ILFI office space in the making.

team). As we gazed up at this enormous document, the scope of what we had chosen to take on by pursuing the Living Building Challenge began to sink in.

Denis Hayes, CEO at the Bullitt Foundation, organizer of the first Earth Day, and noted environmental advocate famously called on the design team to create an "irresistible staircase." The spectacular result of that challenge has been known by this moniker ever since! The stairs' wood treads contributed a bright amber tone to the more dominant metal and glass, showing us how small adjustments in materials can shift the entire experience of being in the space. Hampshire CFO Mark Spiro took one look at the wood treads and said, "We should have these — they are beautiful." Jason Forney added "Somehow, we all flowed from place to place despite record low Seattle temperatures, in a

fifteen-passenger van, found good local beer, savored fresh fish, and learned so much," crediting Carl for leading the way on that important journey of discovery and team building.

Carl did not describe himself as an environmental advocate going into the R.W. Kern Center project. He was a civil engineer born in Illinois, with strong personal ethics and values. He was brought to Hampshire to work through a backlog of projects that simply could not be advanced by such a small staff. There was a lot to do, and Carl's energy revealed itself in many ways, including a nearly daily distance running commitment. The R.W. Kern Center was a glimmer on the horizon when he first arrived at the College. Little did he know that in the summer of 2014, just a few months after the Seattle trip, he would be orchestrating a redesign of the entire core campus.

At 52,000 square feet, the six-story Bullitt Center more than raised the bar for what was possible in the Living built environment.

TOP:
Bullitt Center President Denis Hayes introduces the Hampshire team to the composters that serve the building's toilets.

LEFT:
Getting oriented with Denis Hayes at the ILFI headquarters, with Hampshire College students and staff.

Before school reopened that fall, he had to get the cars and asphalt out of central campus and make way for meadows, a grass common reminiscent of New England towns, and the R.W. Kern Center.

Once construction began at the R.W. Kern Center and Carl could see it taking shape, he quietly transformed into a green building enthusiast. The building tutored him, and everyone else, in the ways of living systems. "Most of us never think about the water we use. It's there, we flush, and it goes away. Well, it turns out there is no 'away.' Everything we do has consequences," commented Carl. His passion and commitment continued to expand to an even deeper conviction.

Carl's Living Building Challenge initiation was swift and thorough, by immersion. When the details of the electrical

contractor's proposed lighting control system came forward, for example, Carl pulled the team to a halt. "We don't need this," he declared. "We want the users to take responsibility for providing the light they need and controlling the power they use. All of us are becoming dependent on unnecessary technology. A sustainable future is personal, starting with turning off the lights." Carl thrives on practicality and elegant execution. "We have lost the ability to design and make large wood buildings, and we need to regain those skills," he said. "Look at this place! We're getting it back. We need to change that default setting of concrete and steel that we see all the time."

As the building construction advanced, Carl began to talk to visitors about how the Living Building Challenge prohibits combustion technologies. "If we burn oil, we have to remember

LEFT:
Inside the irresistible staircase.

TOP:
Bullitt Center workspace.

the BP spill. If we burn gas, we have to carry the burden and damage of fracking."

"We take so much for granted, with all the resources we have," Carl reflected. "I have become more and more aware of this inequity, both in this country and around the world, as a result of the materials sourcing expectations of the Living Building Challenge."

Because of Carl's many responsibilities at Hampshire, he couldn't spend as much time as he would have liked on the R.W. Kern Center. "I spent perhaps one quarter of the time on this project that I might have in another highly controlled setting," he said.

"That's because the team had developed trust and self-reliance. Everything about the way the job was being run reflected care, full ownership, pride, and personal investment. Carl credits his construction and design team (and never his own leadership) with the success. "In all these years, I have never worked with a team so committed to the project, the mission, with such ownership at all levels. It was like they were watching their own money being spent."

LEFT: The watershed at the Federal Building.

BELOW: The Bertschi School Science Wing Living Building was on the tour. Note rainwater drainage routed through the floor in a "runnell."

TOP:
Reused structural timber provides warmth and a fascinating story for the Seattle Federal Building.

NEAR RIGHT:
Carl Weber arranged a visit to the Seattle Federal Building that houses the Army Corps of Engineers regional office. It is a reused industrial site, where more than four hundred thousand board feet of timber was repurposed. The interior represents a replica of the Columbia River watershed!

FAR RIGHT:
Jason Jewhurst of Bruner/Cott climbs past the Bertschi School living wall.

Bill Kern and Leona Kern gaze south out over the Hampshire College campus from the Tardis Room at the R.W. Kern Center.

The Roofer

PAT COFFEY, OUR PAINTING CONTRACTOR FOR BOTH THE R.W. KERN CENTER AND THE HITCHCOCK CENTER FOR THE ENVIRONMENT, WAS CHATTING IN THE R.W. KERN CENTER job trailer with Foreman John Averill one Tuesday after the regular job meeting. Pat kept looking over at the guy standing in the corner smiling. He had greying hair, blue eyes, slightly nicer blue jeans than what are usually worn on the site, work boots, and a project-signature yellow hard hat. Pat was sure he recognized the man but couldn't place him.

Finally, Pat turned to him and asked, "Aren't you the roofer?"

"No," the mystery companion said. "I'm Bill."

After Bill left, John started laughing and turned to Pat. "That's Bill Kern. You know, as in the R.W. Kern Center?"

Even though he is a smart and accomplished man, Pat told me later he felt like a bit of a fool, worried what impression he might have given Bill about the people working on the building that bears his family's name. "Boy did I feel like a donkey. I bet he's thinking, 'We have some really sharp people on this job!'"

Bill gradually became a quiet member of the team, and part of the place. This guy just didn't look the part of a donor, whatever that looks like, because donors don't come and hang out in job trailers and ask questions about fiber optics and solar transformers. They don't stare at stone work as if in meditation. They don't often know a lot about building.

At first, I was emphatic that I did not want Bill in our trailer meetings. I had been leery of his wanting to come to the job site and watch us make our weekly breakfast scramble of half-baked questions, undercooked answers and, by the way, what's burning up on the materials "hot list," the stuff that's required right away. We needed our huddle-time with cider donuts, dry roasted almonds, and mediocre coffee. As the months passed and Bill came up to Amherst every few weeks just to watch and learn, we realized that he was completely our friend and admirer. He began to build genuine friendships with people all across the crews, in every trade.

"One cold and grey winter morning I showed up unannounced at the building site while they were pouring the foundation. John Averill invited me into the construction trailer to warm up and for a cup of green tea. That was the start of a conversation that went on for the next year and a half. Every few weeks when I arrived at the site, John patiently explained to me what was going on during that phase of construction. After a few more visits, each time borrowing a Wright Builders helmet, John told me to keep the helmet, which I still have." Bill recounts,

On that day, and many other days when Bill added grace notes to the music we were all creating, the R.W. Kern Center became more than a project. It became a kind of living incantation. First, it honors Ralph Kern. But it also stands to inspire everyone else within its contact range, embodying our deepest hopes for sustainability and for life itself.

Every one of us has had a dear friend or parent whom we would love to honor. Bill was on that job site to honor his father, R.W. "Ralph" Kern. The more time he spent with us, the better we understood what he appreciated about his father and the stronger our collective bond grew, as fellow travelers on this journey. Together, we were all there to make a building and fulfill a vision. We could see what it meant to Bill to observe our process along the way; that what we did had moment-to-moment meaning for him. The building was more a reflection than a monument.

Bill had come to Hampshire College as a student interested in film and video in the fall of 1975. When he had visited the previous fall with his parents, his father had turned to Bill and said, "I think you would do well here. You have my blessing." That blessing resonated through the four decades that followed, ultimately leading to the R.W. Kern Center's genesis.

Ralph Kern grew up in the Bronx, the son of a cabinet maker who took his son to the shop on Saturday mornings. He and his sister shared a one-bedroom apartment with their parents. He met his true love, Leona from Brooklyn, when they were both students at New York University. After Ralph and Lee were married, they moved to Chelsea, the first in either of their families to live in Manhattan.

Ralph started his career as a broker for the firm of Pease and Edelman, working the core of Manhattan. He worked at putting together the hard deals at the edges, the ones that the big, established players sloughed off. Gradually, he built

his own portfolio and assembled a remarkable real estate business. As their success grew, he told Lee that he was happy to give to worthy causes but he was not interested in the public side of philanthropy; "I don't go to dinners," he used to say. He'd rather go sailing or hang out with his beloved dog, Valkyrie, named in honor of one of his favorite operas.

Ralph and Lee passed on their love of opera to Bill, who, after learning that John Averill was also a fan, arranged to have John and his family join the Kerns at New York's Lincoln Center for Puccini's Tosca. This typifies the Kerns' generosity and reflects their personal interest in the project and its people.

Over time, those of us on the R.W. Kern Center job site would hear bits and pieces of stories about Ralph. Bill and Lee talked of Ralph's hardscrabble life as a builder, which made him seem more like us. One day, Bill looked at the masonry walls gradually taking shape and said, almost dreamily, "My dad would have loved this!" Still, Bill sometimes referred to Ralph's fiscal prudence. As the project budget unfolded, Bill once said ruefully, "I'm glad my dad isn't here to see these numbers!"

Bill was a veteran of some pretty tough project meetings on New York construction sites, and he found our collaborative style both startling and refreshing. At one point he told me, "You know Jonathan, if I had known that construction could be like this, I might have changed careers." What I could not articulate at the time was how the implicit trust and expressed excitement coming from Bill actually changed the figurative pH of the project. His engagement moved it to neutral, away from industry-habitual acidic.

LEFT:
Day breaks at the R. W. Kern Center on Ralph W. Kern's birthday.

TOP:
The R&R Windows team begin their day in midwinter at dawn.

Having Bill on the site became a joy. We looked forward to his visits, not just as a patron but as a valued and respected friend.

Bill asked John Averill in the winter of 2016 about getting into the building early in the morning. He was astonished that he was quickly given the lock combinations and key access to a secure job site. On a cold and windy Monday, February 22, 2016, under grey skies, Bill came up to the Hampshire College campus to mark his father's birthday seven years after his death. He entered the closed-in R.W. Kern Center alone, well before dawn and worked his way to the east side of the building.

He would say a prayer facing east, towards Jerusalem, for his dad, as is the tradition. "Prayer is making a space to feel emotion; to feel the spirit," Bill remarked later. He had chosen the small conference room on the southeast corner of the building, eventually named the "Tardis Room," architecturally unique because it pokes out of the skin of the building, with glass wrapping the south and easterly sides outside of the structural posts and beams.

The sun rose over Mount Norwottuck just as Bill completed his prayers. As it was in deep winter, the sun rose from the southeast, blazing directly into the corner of the room. Bill said it was like "being at Stonehenge at midsummer." The light came quickly once it cleared the craggy mountain outcrops. The

construction trucks began to rumble onto the site. Just after dawn, the beep-beep of the scissor lift could be heard outside the window. Up it came, carrying Jesse Sheldon and his crew from R&R Window Contractors, to complete the setting of the glass.

Imagining Bill's voice quietly finding its way into corners of that room in a building being born, on a mission to celebrate rebirth still gives me chills. On that day, and many other days when Bill added grace notes to the music we were all creating, the R.W. Kern Center became more than a project. It became a kind of living incantation. First, it honors Ralph Kern. But it also stands to inspire everyone else within its contact range, embodying our deepest hopes for sustainability and for life itself.

The building that day was becoming much more than a roof over Bill's head. As I would learn later from Hampshire College students studying the Living Building Challenge, when it comes to the core message, the roof is really the foundation of the building's sustainability. It embodies two of the required petals: Water and Energy to sustain not only the building itself, but all other life surrounding it. Maybe, then, a building is all the things, including prayer, that hold up the roof. If the roof is central not only to shelter but to the survival of the planet, through its contributions of water and energy, then maybe Bill really was the roofer after all.

The R.W. Kern Center at Hampshire College, looking southwest.

How Two Buildings Found Their Rightful Places

"HOME IS THE PLACE WHERE, WHEN YOU HAVE TO GO THERE, THEY HAVE TO TAKE YOU IN," AMHERST, MASSACHUSETTS legend and poet Robert Frost once notably wrote. But where does a *building* really belong? How do we come to know its rightful place in the landscape and circumstances of its place? What is the alchemy of belonging, necessity, and destiny that produces a building in its place?

The siting of a building is typically the professional purview of architects and landscape architects. Yet, builders spend so many months working in and transforming a place that, experientially, we are creating that habitat. We have an up-close relationship with it and, in the case of a Living Building, can watch and feel its mission come to life. This is a profound experience and a source of honor reserved for makers.

Siting a building is expressed in terms of functions, traffic considerations, emergency access, pedestrian safety, proximity to utilities, drainage, permitting, sound abatement from adjoining buildings or functions, views, solar orientation, and more. But how does the building and its mission propel it toward the particular location, orientation, and relationship within the context of the rest of the built and natural landscape it inhabits?

For Living Buildings, the care required in siting is deep and wide. Beyond the practical considerations are certain expectations: a place that harmonizes with nature, provides food, and expresses biophilia (our natural affinity for nature) — all in a car-free environment if at all possible. Avoiding displacement of agriculture is critical.

After nearly fifty years in various make-do locations around Amherst, the award-winning educational programs of the Hitchcock Center for the Environment desperately needed new,

larger, and better space. For years they had been in buildings on a beautiful town-owned reserve just south of the town center. But the space was cramped, and staff would joke in cold weather about providing mammal habitat between the poorly insulated floor joists under the classroom that was built on piers. Some suggested that with the addition of Plexiglas panels in the floor, skunk hibernation could become an exhibit! Staff were piled up on top of each other in nooks and crannies, which in turn were piled with documents, materials, formaldehyde-laden stuffed animals and birds. It was lively and cozy, and also limiting and maddeningly inefficient.

In 2011, shortly before Jonathan Lash began his tenure as the sixth president of Hampshire College, less than three miles down the road from the Hitchcock Center, a meeting of the minds rekindled the prospects for a partnership and led to an agreement. The possible relocation of the Hitchcock Center to Hampshire had been on and off the table for some years,

HAMPSHIRE, THEN AND NOW

In the mid-1960s, the Hampshire College campus was assembled from, and carved out of, beautiful western Massachusetts farmland, pasture, woodlands, and apple orchards. Its western borders encompass some of what was shoreline during the post glacial lakes that filled the valley during aboriginal times. The terrain and eco systems are varied and abundant, and the view of the Mount Holyoke Range, with its basalt uplift core, is breathtaking.

The northern border section of the campus was revived for science and agriculture early in the College's life in the 1970s. Active farming, and farm programming, began in the 1980s. Over time, as farm programs integrated into the curriculum and interests in sustainable agriculture grew, the Farm Center became a signature feature of the campus and the Hampshire education. Several sections of the campus had been apple orchards at one time or another and continued to be farmed up into the 1970s, even after the College opened. These orchards provided apples for eating and baking, as well as for the mash used in Atkins Farms' legendary cider, pressed from the blemished apple drops into the rich sweet murky russet jugs of juice that are a signature of autumn in New England. Atkins Farms still makes cider today.

but now, with Lash as president, and with the help of Hampshire Trustee Kenneth Rosenthal and faculty member Larry Winship, Hitchcock's Executive Director Julie Johnson had found willing and eager collaborators.

Upon his arrival at Hampshire, Lash had immediately understood that furthering Hampshire College's environmental mission would be strengthened by having the Center near the campus, and the Center would draw a new range of visitors and constituencies from the College's network. This historic farm-turned-college was the perfect host for the Hitchcock Center. A ninety-nine-year land lease was put in place.

The farm was one of the places on campus where people could make things and do manual work, above and beyond research and conversation. Students tramped through the fields, across paths and wooded glens between the residential campus and the farm. Every day, they passed through the overgrown thickets on what would become the home for the Hitchcock Center.

The new Hitchcock Center would need to be accessible and visible from Highway 116 for car, bus, bike, and foot traffic. It would need to have utilities, public water for fire suppression, and, for mission reasons, not substantially disrupt or diminish agricultural programs and resources. It would need to be a place that became its own destination for learning about the environment, and for experiencing the peaceful and majestic beauty that is threatened every day by human activity.

Hampshire Farm Center staff wanted to preserve the existing pasture for livestock and haying, so the siting options had to meet that criterion. For the Hitchcock Center itself, proximity to Hampshire's 640-acre campus was enticing, but adjacency to varied habitat for education was also very important. They were still fond of their pond at the old place, with its delicious assortment of mud, bugs, turtles, and frogs. Generations of children had learned there and gone home wet, filthy, happy, and tired. Residents of the region who would become key to funding the new location fondly remembered their childhood times at the Hitchcock Center.

All was not bucolic, however, as fruit growing and modern agricultural chemistry intersected after World War II. The growth of agri-business exploded and chemicals for pests and fertilizer became ubiquitous. Apples were required to be sprayed for pest control and consumers came to expect nearly perfect fruit. The froth for spraying apples was a deadly one, laced with arsenic to kill the bugs and lead to make the poison stick to the fruit.

Lead arsenate was sprayed on the trees and dripped off the fruit and foliage onto the ground at the leaf-canopy rim. Although the compound was not water-soluble, it also didn't degrade, remaining on the chosen Hitchcock site long after the trees had died and decomposed.

The concentrations of these chemicals were not technically reportable for commercial purposes, such as developing a shopping center, but only barely acceptable for residential use. Because children would play in the soil at the new Hitchcock Center, and gardens would be made of it, it became necessary to remediate the soils to end any possible claims and health worries regarding soil contamination. It was not possible to map the actual location of historic trees and the soil test concentration of contaminants varied considerably across the site. But contaminants were everywhere. Geotechnical engineers determined that about nine inches of soil would need to be removed and disposed of.

Upon his arrival at Hampshire, Lash had immediately understood that furthering Hampshire College's environmental mission would be strengthened by having the Center near the campus, and the Center would draw a new range of visitors and constituencies from the College's network.

Practical gardeners wondered if, by tilling twelve inches of soil, the concentrations could be reduced and in effect diluted to tolerable levels. But the level of spot-contamination made any such approach impossible. It clearly required a specified, protected, and controlled process of remediation.

Bioremediation plans and research, using microbial action, came up negative. Failing that, the prospect of excavating and hauling more than one hundred eighteen-wheel dump truck loads of tainted material to a distant disposal site was daunting. The thought of diverting 10 percent of the Hitchcock Center's four-million-dollar construction budget toward hauling and replacing topsoil was even more frightening. Where would such material go? Into whose neighborhood? What risks lay hidden at a practical level for handling and transportation? Against this backdrop of a now-determined overall site location tucked into the edge of the old orchards and out of the hayfields came the big question of "What now?"

Geotechnical engineers Mike Talbot and Ashley Sullivan determined that it could be possible to encapsulate the tainted soils underground and build up mats of crushed stone and other base materials on top of them to support the parking areas.

So, while the building could not be located in this area, as the materials buried would not be suitable for structural bearing, unpaved parking on top was possible.

It is by no means standard practice to place organic materials underneath bearing substrate materials, but that is exactly the strategy that geotechnical engineers devised. The spoils did not have to be hauled hundreds of miles away. This on-site encapsulation reduced the remediation costs from more than $400,000 to about $60,000, and also led us to eliminate blacktop from the parking area because the base was potentially unstable.

The Hitchcock Center building would now settle into the north side of the site, much preferred by the whole team. The visitor entrance would be on the sunny south façade, where it is warmer in winter and the solar panels are in full view. Even the parking area serves as a teaching tool, with parking spots that are smaller and fewer, bollards of invasive but durable native black locust, and crushed stone surface in lieu of blacktop.

The building would come to nestle into the old woods and brush, peek out into the meadow, to stand guard over the Pelham Hills and the Holyoke Range, witness every sunrise, and join a scattering of older farm buildings housing campus offices and services. Those older buildings also remind every visitor that the site is a long-inhabited rural place — open fields and dense brush

FAR LEFT:
Deep in the overgrown old orchard this double tree in the form of an "H", designated for both Hampshire and Hitchcock, grew in its implausible and brilliant formation.

LEFT:
Heritage apple trees still hung on, even as birds flew freely through them.

RIGHT:
Mist shrouded Pelham Hills form the easterly prospect from the Hitchcock Center.

Those older buildings also remind every visitor that the site is a long-inhabited rural place — open fields and dense brush once farmed by Europeans and, long before, roamed, inhabited, and treasured by native people since the melting of the last ice nearly 12,000 years ago.

once farmed by Europeans and, long before, roamed, inhabited, and treasured by native people since the melting of the last ice nearly 12,000 years ago.

....

"Why do we have a fossil fuel spear into the heart of the campus?" pondered President Jonathan Lash, as he observed the wide, straight roadway that came up to a cul-de-sac in front of the Hampshire College Harold F. Johnson Library. Here, just a quarter mile away from the Hitchcock Center site, a different story was unfolding.

The obvious answers to Lash's query included "Because it's there" and "Because it's expensive to move." But those answers weren't good enough; a process to re-envision the core campus was ignited. The 1960s suburban design by Sasaki Associates was typical for the time, and its transformation into a walkable meadow signified the broad sweep of change envisioned. The R.W. Kern Center would stand at the heart of that vision.

The R.W. Kern Center's proposed site was awkward in its inward and outward connections to the landscape. It was separated from other core campus buildings by a major road, placing it in close proximity to cars and idling diesel buses. The College's campus planner, Rick Klein, from Berkshire Design Group in Northampton, prepared a scheme for relocating cars to the perimeter of the core campus, and converting the areas rescued from vehicles into sweeping meadows and lawn. The R.W. Kern Center site could now slip over closer to the Robert Crown Center (RCC) recreation facility, placing it more centrally on campus and strengthening its accessibility via foot and bicycle transportation.

Creating Sustainable Buildings That Renew Our World

A CAMPUS TRANSFORMED

Looking west across the core academic buildings of the Hampshire College campus toward the Berkshire hills beyond. This grass and wild flower meadow replaces the old center campus road. Behind the R.W. Kern Center is the Robert Crown Center, then the Harold Johnson Library. Straight ahead is the Cole Science Center, with Franklin Patterson Hall off to the left.

While it is true that the architecture of the Hampshire College campus is eclectic and varied beyond its farmhouse and agrarian roots, it is, in the main, brick and concrete built in the 1960s and 1970s during an era of seventeen-cent fuel oil and nuclear-powered electricity predicted to be too cheap to bother metering.

Hampshire was built late enough in the mid-twentieth century to take advantage of positive building trends: elevators were becoming more common, lead and asbestos were disappearing from building materials, insulated glass was the norm, and air-conditioning was often standard. These were not particularly green standards, to be sure, but resulted in sturdy and very serviceable structures that were well positioned for the future.

In the early 1980s, the Robert Crown Center was added to the campus. With pool and gym facilities, the "RCC" was skinned in a scored concrete block and introduced the first real angled surfaces to the core campus buildings. But it lacked architectural reference to the square, muscular nature of the campus architecture and got a bit lost at the northeast corner of the main quad, tenuously connected to the library by an overhead bridge.

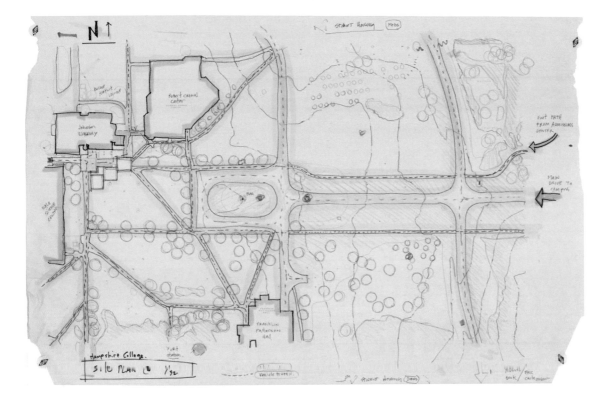

The Bruner/Cott team
sketched the existing
Hampshire College core
campus in preparation for
its transformation.

The advent of the R.W. Kern Center established new connections. Now, the angular and once-orphaned RCC has another angled building for proximal company, as well as R.W. Kern Center detailing that references the earlier original campus architecture through some precast concrete trim components. Beyond that, the R.W. Kern Center's dramatic form opens to the land, the view, the College, and the future.

The grounds around the R.W. Kern Center include wild flower meadows and some mowed areas for outdoor gathering. The College chooses not to maintain meticulous landscape details in all locations. Rather, those detailed efforts are focused in a few locations, leaving much of the rest to meadow, bark mulch, and natural abundance.

Nature helps define the R.W. Kern Center's home. With an Ashfield schist stone exterior interrupted by grey pre-cast concrete bands and capped with wall panels and soffit in tawny Atlantic white cedar from within 250 miles, the building is made almost entirely of locally-sourced materials.

The R.W. Kern Center found its rightful place, insisting on where it needed to be and shouldering its way through tons of bituminous concrete. I have walked and dawdled there to absorb how the building derives itself from the campus while also taking it in a new direction. It does not set a new standard of how things should or will look; instead, it poses questions of possibility and embraces the landscape and views, opening the gates of the journey. The R.W. Kern Center invites curiosity without demanding adherence. It quietly insists on engagement and enthusiasm.

For both the Hitchcock Center and the R.W. Kern Center, Living Building aspiration means finding the rightful place in the landscape, the right orientation, and the right kinds of connections to place. Each building expresses its designer's commitment to create a distinct, dramatic, transformative, and unobtrusive place.

Four Scientists Walk into a Diner

FOUR SCIENCE AND MATH COLLEAGUES FROM HAMPSHIRE COLLEGE WALKED INTO THE BUSY METRO CAFÉ DINER IN Atlanta, surrounded by the looks and smells of fresh-cooked bacon, home fries, and grits awash in butter. Preparing to reenter the no-daylight realm of the "Transforming STEM in Higher Education" conference, they took a booth and ordered up. Together, they brought to the table compelling passions for microbes, calculus, groundwater, and slime.

Jason Tor, the microbiologist, wondered how they could they use the College's new Living Building to teach science. "It's going to be full of interesting systems for water and waste and energy," he said. Not to be left out, Sarah Hews, professor of mathematics, remarked with a characteristic twinkle in her eye, "You know, everything comes back to calculus. We can use mathematical models to understand what's going on. The students will do projects and find themselves using calculus before they know it."

"I was very excited by the conversation! It seemed like a great new idea, and an opportunity to collaborate and learn from each other. We were talking a lot about community, and about attracting students to the sciences in their first year of college," remarked Jason Tor.

They began to talk about how the R.W. Kern Center's greywater waste stream would work, since, as Tor likes to say, "Microbes do all the world's work." Professor Christina Cianfrani, a hydrologist, was keen to understand all aspects of the water system, from rooftop collection to storage, and especially the waste stream and groundwater impacts. Megan Dobro, professor of biology, was also there for this lively discussion.

Over the next sixty minutes, surrounded by the remains of eggs, muffins, and grits, they mapped out a collaborative model for teaching first-year college students to engage critical scientific and environmental questions using the not-yet-constructed R.W.

Biomimicry at work. Seven tortilla chip petals in huevos rancheros inaugurate what might have become known as the Large Breakfast Challenge at the Metro Café Diner.

Kern Center. They would each have seminars, and at least once every week the groups would get together and students would form collaborative project teams. By modeling truly collaborative teaching about issues they were still exploring in their own research, professors would expose these students fresh out of high school to the exciting mysteries of unexplored science and the dynamics of human interaction with the environment. All this through a building. Not just any building, but a Living Building designed and conceived to carry an abundant embedded message of curiosity.

Professor Cianfrani remarked that, as Hampshire teachers, they were encouraged to take risks and explore new areas of study. "Promotion and reappointment guidelines reward this. Our spirits are free to follow the students' interest, our own passions, and the data from the building itself as it is collected."

In the particularly bitter winter of 2014-2015, while Wright Builders and the rest of the project team was slogging it out as to what materials we could use and how to ensure that the construction quality exceeded the energy modeling by a healthy

By modeling truly collaborative teaching about issues they were still exploring in their own research, professors would expose these students fresh out of high school to the exciting mysteries of unexplored science and the dynamics of human interaction with the environment. All this through a building. Not just any building, but a Living Building designed and conceived to carry an abundant embedded message of curiosity.

margin, students were getting ready to understand energy modeling with the help of Earth Sciences Professor Steven Roof. Would it really be possible for this very busy building, almost a transit station on the campus, to conserve its energy effectively enough to reach net zero annual consumption? Over the next several years, students and faculty would examine all parts of the building, culminating in a project to record and document the building's actual energy usage.

Who knew that copiers and printers use more than half their daily energy during sleep mode? Who knew that an espresso machine uses half its daily energy just keeping the water reservoir warm so baristas can start up on two minutes' notice? First-year Hampshire students, working with Professor Roof, figured this out.

Witnessing this student and faculty engagement was powerful for Jason Forney, project architect. "So many institutions aspire to use a new building as a teaching tool, but everyday life somehow conspires against this goal," he said. "For Hampshire, curiosity is just in their blood." Like professors who want their students to be excited and grow, builders and architects want their buildings to DO something, SAY something, CREATE something. All living things communicate, even Jason Tor's tiny, heroic microbes; it's just that most of the time we are not listening.

After the building opened, Todd Holland, Hampshire's staff mechanical engineer, was listening closely, not only to the messages from the greywater system but to his voicemails, all pointing to the same curious thing: a sweet, ripe, smell was beginning to pervade the R.W. Kern Center, especially in the wide open, naturally lit atrium area where everyone gathers, meets, connects, and passes through.

LEFT: Hampshire College Farm pigs thrive on leftovers of dairy from the Kern Kafé, as well as lots of dining hall treats.

ABOVE: **Friendly critters too!**

Visiting days were at hand, so this was a mystery that needed to be solved. In other institutions, heads might have rolled because the building was not at tip-top spit and polish in time for these important events. Instead of panicking, Todd addressed the malodorous issue in a manner that conveyed the project's mission and invited the visitors' curiosity. A note appeared on the north entry door that simply said, "Please excuse the inconvenience. Our research is continuing."

It turned out that the wastewater and coffee from the Kern Kafé, mixed with the end-of-day pour-off of leftover milk and cream, was creating an unmanageable brew of rich nutrients. When these circulated through the drip irrigation hoses in the planters, things began to go sour. Very sour. The solution was to catch solids in a used piece of nylon stocking and save all the leftover dairy for the pigs down at the Hampshire College Farm.

Every human action affects the surrounding natural systems, either positively or negatively. In this case, the impact of our intervention was apparent within a few days. We couldn't turn away, shrug, or set the issue aside for another day. Our responsibility as conservators was to dig in, all the way, right away.

This solution was another step in the research that began as a breakfast conversation in Atlanta, with faculty looking for a fresh way to connect with students and with each other. From that yearning for adventure and community came curricula for several disciplines within natural sciences and mathematics. In 2017, the four scientists received a grant to travel and see other Living Buildings, and to develop a broad-based national curriculum around Living Buildings.

Jason Tor told me, "You know, I used to wish that someday we would get a new science building. Then I realized, with the R.W. Kern Center, we already had one!"

Creating Sustainable Buildings That Renew Our World

Special Delivery

KELLY ARD HAIGH'S WATER BROKE ON FEBRUARY 6, 2015; LABOR FOR HER FIRSTBORN WAS GETTING UNDERWAY in earnest just a tiny bit earlier than expected. After a hospital visit, where she and her husband were told to come back later in the day, she called Sam Batchelor, her partner at designLAB architects, with the news that she would be missing from the Hitchcock Center for the Environment project for a few months.

"I went home and sent out a nice long coordination email to all the consultants to make sure everyone knew that Sam was going to take it across the finish line after all," Kelly reported. "I redlined a set of drawings to capture everything that was on my to-do list for that final week. Sam came over that afternoon (I was having only mild contractions at that point) to review the set and all outstanding coordination issues." Kelly and Sam spread out the nearly finished set of construction drawings for the Hitchcock Center and went to work.

The design process had lasted more than two years and Kelly's baby had been gestating for nearly nine months. There was a beautiful alignment here; the documents would be finished by February 13th and her due date was the 16th. It's just that Baby Lakin changed his travel arrangements and arrived ten days early.

To the construction team, the progression of final design documents all seemed charmed and seamless. The drawings were done, Kelly had her baby, and we got the set we needed. I didn't know until about three years later that Kelly's determination to fully complete and coordinate an exceptionally thorough set of drawings had not quite gone as planned. She was deeply focused on the project during those last months,

and then Sam stepped in and made the most of the final week of the process while Kelly got on with the business of new parenting. "Sam came back over to my house after Lakin was born so we could do a final review together before issuing the set to you guys at Wright Builders," she later told me.

A powerful gestational and birth message is strongly embedded in the process of designing or constructing any building. Kelly had lived and breathed the Hitchcock Center for years. She felt the pulse of the place; how it needed to be a safe harbor, an interface between the outside and the inside worlds, both architecturally and figuratively, for each visitor. "The building needs to present balance and harmony," Kelly said. In addition to her professional perceptiveness, she embodied a deep curiosity and enthusiasm throughout the design process.

OPPOSITE:
Kelly Ard Haigh's son, Lakin, gets his first look at his mom's design showplace, the Hitchcock Center for the Environment.

RIGHT:
Architect Kelly Ard Haigh of designLAB architects looks up from her work table in Boston.

After having been taught by the Hitchcock Center educators about their work, the design team collaborated to develop what they called an "architectural pedagogy." The building would be a dynamic partner in the teaching and learning that occurred within its walls. After the teachers had done a presentation session for the design team, Kelly and Sam brought out several of their key consultants to meet with the staff. "Our consultants got to see first-hand how the teachers worked; how passionate they were about the building as a tool and a laboratory," Kelly reported. "We were used to having them meet with facilities staff members at schools and so on, but this was different. These educators remade their curriculum using the building itself."

The consultants' sessions were fun for all of us. All we had to do was pay attention and learn. Kelly and Sam had changed the process, and through the shift let everyone know this was not business as usual. All the while, the teachers were soaking up the building science and design concepts. This new knowledge would reappear in the curriculum as a focus on engineering and materials when the Center opened in its new home in September 2016.

For Kelly, the Hitchcock Center's Living Building stands as much more than a design project. The work integrated all of her personal skills, design talents, and values, creating a deep level of ownership for all facets of the project. "I really love the interrelated memory of Lakin's and Hitchcock's deliveries," she said. Special, indeed.

Creating Sustainable Buildings That Renew Our World

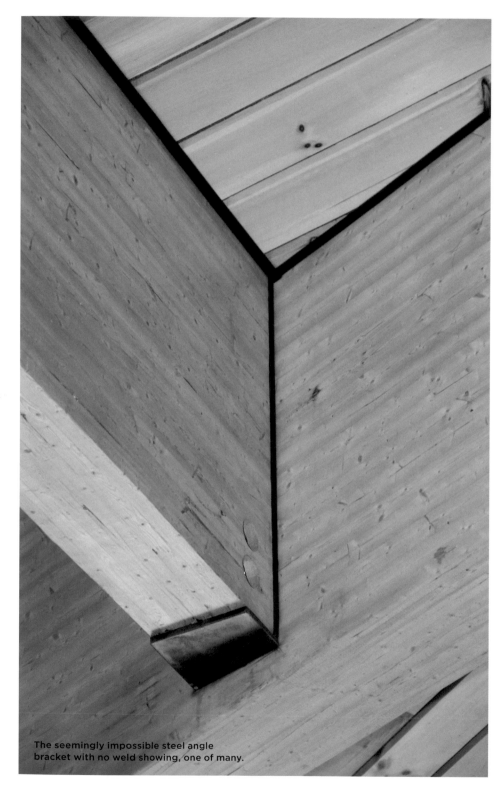

44

The seemingly impossible steel angle
bracket with no weld showing, one of many.

First
Tour,
Second
Floor

CHUCK KEPT LOOKING
AROUND AT THE NEWLY
ERECTED POSTS AND BEAMS
rising up into the pure blue expanse above.
He lightly tugged at my sleeve, pulled me to
the side, and pointed up at a hanger bracket
joining a horizontal beam to a post. It was a
perfectly square "L" joint. "How did they do
that?" he asked. "What is holding it together?"
I looked more closely. I was about to say that
it was bent or forged, but that couldn't be true
— it was a perfectly square right-angle joint
with no evident fillet of welding material to
hold it together. How? I realized I was just as
stumped as my guest. "I don't know, Chuck,
but it seems to be holding!" I quipped.

I led a group of friends of the College up the
temporary stairs for our first group tour to
the second floor of the R.W. Kern Center. We
were there on a day when the sky was the color
of stone-washed denim and the mountains
were leafed out in late-spring green. The
first of the timbers had been raised above the
second floor, gesturing to the roof line with
their tips, crossbeams in place. Otherwise,
we were open to the sky with only the barest
of wood members crossing in space.

This characteristic of embodied strength, like the steel work with its meticulous and mysterious connections, reflects the ways that craftsmanship, workmanship, engineering, and design create a unified message of sustainable and inspired construction.

Everyone affiliated with Hampshire College knows Charles Longsworth as "Chuck." On that late spring afternoon in 2015, the College's first employee and second president, now in his early eighties, stood on the upper floor deck along with his wife, Polly, still entranced by the place they did so much to create. Only it was not really their first tour. They were the only ones among us to have been here before. Chuck remembers building an observation platform not far from this location out of donated power poles during early construction of the College in 1969.

No one except swooping, migrating, and passing birds had ever seen the College from this particular location and perspective. We stood still in what would become the admissions presentation room, facing the campus and the mountains beyond. A hush fell over the group as we scanned the near and distant terrain, surrounded by tiny whispers of breeze. The conversation resumed in small groups as we absorbed the majesty of the view and place. Meaning and opportunity seemed to come alive in the moment. The drifting clouds made us feel like the building was in motion.

Back to Chuck's question: it's relatively common for me not to have the answer. That's part of the adventure and the excitement. The working men and women are constantly fulfilling design ideas and engineering expectations, figuring out the puzzles. No one is omnipotent and everyone is sharing their discoveries with everyone else.

The Monday after my first tour of the second floor with Chuck, I asked "CJ" Brehio, the foreman from New Hampshire-based Bensonwood, our timber frame fabricators and installers, about the detail. There was a weld fillet in there all right, CJ said, but it stopped about a half-inch from each end of the joint. The corner of the wood beams had been beveled off to clear the weld, but the bevel back-cut stopped just short of each end. A beautiful sleight of hand. Every beam seat on all floors of the building had been detailed this way to ensure a seemingly impossible square corner and crisp detailing. The meeting of warm and cool, fiber and ore. Chuck was incredulous at the effort and skill when I told him about it. What struck me even more than Chuck's curiosity was his eye for detail and precision — powerful proof that he valued the work of this structure's makers.

The powerful and visible structure demonstrates its form and strength both through the sheer size of the timbers and through their majestic patterns and connections. The wood itself, laminated from small pieces of spruce that would once have been considered scrap, made us look more closely and examine how the beam material is glued up. This is not old-growth irreplaceable wood, but rather a laminate of small pieces from the heart, or pith, of black spruce. The tree grows slowly in eastern Canada, has many small pin knots but very few large defects. Cut open one of these laminated timbers and you will find that the material, even when invisible, is solid and beautiful.

This characteristic of embodied strength, like the steel work with its meticulous and mysterious connections, reflects the ways that craftsmanship, workmanship, engineering, and design create a unified message of sustainable and inspired construction. For the builders and makers, this confluence reflects the same underlying values inherent in all regenerative design — it's our way of joining in, joining hands in the work, and saying "yes!"

**Original watercolor
by Jan Ruby Crystal**

Back in the 1960s, Chuck and Polly had bounced around in their
VW microbus through what were then the fields and apple orchards
of South Amherst. When they squinted, they could imagine the
college that would eventually take root on this spot. To this day,
they convey that same wistful and passionate clairvoyance that has
always provided so much inspiration at this young college.

Within three days of the arrival of the first students at the College in the
fall of 1970, Chuck had memorized all 251 student names. (Most of us
were still trying to learn the names of our suitemates!) Before that, Chuck
had engineered the assembly of the College's land, finances, and built
environment. His masterful appreciation of making, as evidenced in the
creation of a college, has endured and thrived in the decades since.

Sandbags simulating record snow and ice conditions ballast the Hitchcock Center gutter mockup, testing what the design software could not model.

Minds and Hands in the Gutter

AN UNGAINLY TWELVE-FOOT-LONG WING-LIKE HULK LOADED WITH SANDBAGS LURKED IN THE WRIGHT BUILDERS CABINET SHOP FOR WEEKS. IT WAS THE answer to a conundrum faced by engineer Erik Anders Nelson from Structures Workshop of how to verify the overhang design for the Hitchcock Center. "I don't have a way to test the engineering for those in my software," he said. These overhangs were a signature element of the design because they create seasonal shading for south-facing glass, collect water, and give the building its inspired winged-butterfly roof shape. "But if you make a full-sized ballasted mock-up and load it with sand bags, we can measure if there is any movement or failure, and that should do it."

Gutters on Living Buildings are more than pipes to dispose of inconvenient water. They are the buildings' major arteries that harvest and distribute water, which, along with air, is necessary for life. True in biology; true in regenerative design.

After Erik suggested the work-around, Hitchcock Center Project Manager Mark Ledwell, Foreman Jim Small, and Wright Builders materials maestro Andrew "Sol" Solem turned their attention to preparing the mock-up of the roof edge system and monitoring the 5000-pound elephant in the room. It was like watching grass grow as, day by day, we kept checking, measuring, and wondering if some morning we would come in and find the whole apparatus collapsed under the weight of some gargantuan, historic simulated snow and ice storm. But it never did.

Most building systems rely on through-connections to assemble and secure the overall structural system. Holding themselves together, staying connected. However, these metal bolts, screws, beams, cleats, and penetrations become what are called thermal bridges because they break the continuity of the insulation barrier. They transmit heat and cold and invite in moisture and condensation. We work every day to eliminate this risk.

Think of the Hitchcock Center's insulated structure as being like a huge refrigerator, with two layers of three-inch reclaimed and repurposed polyisocyanate insulation that wrap around the walls and roof virtually uninterrupted. Over this is a waterproofing membrane of black bituminous sheeting, then sheathing plywood, and then the roofing or siding. It is elegant and efficient as a thermal device, but a bit ungainly to assemble because of the thickness.

The outside plywood skin of the roof underneath the standing seam roof metal is secured down through six inches of insulation to the roof decking planks with seven and one-half-inch screws. This plywood extends past the south edge of the building about eighteen inches, and then is connected by a V-shaped steel plate and screws to an upturned winglet. This winglet and its gutter assembly are in turn supported by elegant built-up cedar timber buttresses braced back to the concrete block piers resting on the foundation footing, but outside of the insulation.

It's just the screws and bolts of that V-plate in the bottom of what would become a giant gutter that is keeping it tethered. Rather than shrugging or stepping aside, Erik's answer was to experiment and test. Builders love actual information, details, and the back-up science. We thrive on confirmation of answers. Being sure that we are building a 100-year product means being proactive, innovative, and taking no unnecessary chances. A resilient building must not buckle under extraordinary weather demands. The result: the finished Hitchcock Center building far exceeds the PassivHaus standard for air infiltration.

The original drawings showed the exterior wall planks being connected to the posts by "lag screws." When Mark Ledwell asked about this, Erik said, "Oh, that's just a suggestion. What would work best for you?" This was typical of the way Sam and Erik handled field questions and detail discussions. Mark

OPPOSITE, TOP:
R.W. Kern Center tapered roof revealing the built-in drainage concept for rainwater collection.

OPPOSITE, BOTTOM:
Rainwater collection piping and systems at the east end of the R.W. Kern Center. The WUSY filter, first flush discharge piping, and exposed reservoir top are shown as they operate in full view in order to tell their story.

RIGHT:
Hitchcock Center solar arrays and water collection gutters, as seen facing west.

proposed using power-driven screws, similar to Timberlok, which were easy to install, flush to the surface when set, and strong.

A quarter mile southeast, at the R.W. Kern Center, architect Christopher Nielsen had drawn an inspired detail for moving the water toward downspouts at either end of the building. It was nothing short of artistic and would be crazy to build. Unlike typical gutters that are added onto the eaves of buildings and slowly pitch toward one end, Christopher and the Bruner/Cott Architects team wanted to make the R.W. Kern Center integral gutters concealed and their pitch integrated into the building design.

Looking up at the eave overhang that shades the upper floor of the building one can see that it is not parallel to the building face. It extends further outward by four or five feet as it heads toward the downspouts at either outboard end. The roof itself has a 1.5/12 pitch; the built-in gutter runs parallel to the eave but not to the building. This gutter has pitch because of the architecture. I did not fully understand this until near the end of framing, but simply assumed Christopher had eschewed yet another straight parallel line in favor of something more difficult and obtuse!

I had seen Foreman John Averill intensely focused on an assembly of laminated microlam beams meeting at a built-up hip rafter designed to carry these overhangs. The structural drawings for the building were basically conceptual, and it fell to John and Project Manager Tom Lucia to figure out how to layer and join and support the various members in and out of compound angles. Once the soffit boards were installed, all that masterful carpentry and mathematics were tucked away like the muscles inside the skin of a body.

Unlike at the Hitchcock Center, these overhangs are cantilevered from the building face and structurally fastened to the side of the roof trusses. Two engineering paradigms meet in mid-air. Truss designer Brian Tetreault at United Forest Products had researched the issue and was able to allow a five-foot overhanging framing member to be affixed to their truss assembly, even though their design software typically rejects those requests.

Creating the taper and its embedded pitch meant that every rafter cantilevered "outlook" beam had a different projection from the building, and its end-cut was ever so slightly both out of

CONCRETE SOLUTIONS

I first met Erik Anders Nelson during training workshops for Hitchcock Center staff on all the main components of good project design. The design consultants themselves presented in three separate three-hour sessions on topics including site design, landscape, and structural engineering. I went to all of the workshops and they were excellent. It was great to be in a room full of educators being educated! Teachers make eager students, appreciative of the connection and process that they have chosen as a career and passion.

Erik had a great raft of slides showing how different kinds of buildings have been structured throughout history. He showed a non-linear inflatable device that can be used to reduce the amount of concrete in a plywood form for a poured beam by leaving out the dead weight parts of the pour. Concrete, he went on to explain, is responsible for generating more than 10 percent of the world's released carbon each year, more than automobiles. So, reducing concrete quantities has a positive environmental outcome.

The points he made were startling. During the presentation, we could hear Erik's voice start to quaver just a little. "Sorry," he said. "When I get excited my voice starts to shake." We looked at each other, touched and enthralled by the excitement of ENGINEERING!

TOP: **The south overhang at the Hitchcock Center provides protected outdoor space, seasonal shading and rainwater collection.**

ABOVE: **Wright Builders Principal Mark Ledwell discusses site development with one of his team members.**

square and tapered. Now imagine attaching each of these slightly different length beams to each of the roof trusses, themselves each different. Each of the 128 beams was formulated to create a roof warp that suggests flight and movement. Back down on the dirt with saws and wood, John Averill dug into the work, focused, skilled, and determined. Today, when we see the R.W. Kern Center from a slight distance, we can see the lift and turn of this wing shape. We can't see the bones in the bird's wing, but we can witness its grace and power. John and the team brought

that elegance to life with thousands of straight sticks of wood assembled to gracefully and unconventionally simulate movement.

The Living Building Challenge demands that we stretch and work together, much like the systems in the structures we are creating. On the campus of Hampshire College, two Living Buildings' shading and water collection systems fuse complex and sometimes opposing structural elements, a testament to their designers and builders who are their family of origin.

SEALING THE DEAL

The cantilever design of the R.W. Kern Center's roof carried other construction detailing challenges. The Prosoco Cat-5 trowel- and roller-applied air vapor barrier on the outside of the building sheathing provided an essential membrane. (For more about the Prosoco Corporation and its relationship with the Living Building Challenge, see "Concrete Revealed.") But the roof system was designed for the truss cavity to be filled with cellulose fiber insulation. This requires the air vapor barrier to transition from the outside of the wall system to the underside of the trusses at the ceiling level.

The structural ceiling is half-inch plywood with the seams taped. The transition is made with a bituminous adhesive sheet that sticks to the Cat-5 on the outside of the wall, wraps up over the top of the wall structure and back under the plywood ceiling, and which has to remain protected against damage throughout the installation of all the roof assemblies. Marc Rosenbaum from South Mountain Company, the energy modeling guru and building envelope consultant on the project, provided detailed assistance on this item, along with a message of urgency in his seemingly mild, voice-never-raised way. John Averill made it happen.

Tale of
Two Drywalls

ON THE SECOND DAY OF BASEMENT DRYWALL INSTALLATION AT THE R.W. KERN CENTER, FOREMAN JOHN AVERILL looked at his phone, and then disappeared quickly down the basement stairs. The whine and grind of drywall screw guns and routers stopped abruptly. Voices murmured.

Just the day before, the project had reached an informal mini-milestone — finish surface materials could begin to come on the site. The basement drywall at R.W. Kern Center needed to be loaded in from above before the first-floor deck planking went on over the small basement area. This sequence would allow us to use longer sheets with fewer seams. Even though it was early on in construction, we were all excited to see some board go up.

The sheetrock had arrived in the morning, and the team of hangers started their work in the afternoon. Scott Belanger, assistant foreman for Wright Builders, was in charge of scanning all the incoming product labels and ensuring total logging of all materials into and out of the site. Bar codes were scanned, processed, and documented.

Several of us were working out of the Wright Builders office twenty minutes away when we received a call. A double-check had been made and there was bad news. The bar code scan from the delivered product did not match the ordered product. We had received the wrong material, from the "other" manufacturing plant. The team was hanging drywall that was not Red List-compliant.

OPPOSITE, LEFT:
Drywallers sculpted their work around emerging conduits.

OPPOSITE, RIGHT:
Framers work to get the R.W. Kern Center ready for the
waiting drywall, now with the correct sourcing.

Office staff called John Averill at the site to give him the update. John initiated a full stop. After he discussed things with the subcontractor, the panels had to be unscrewed, restacked, hoisted out of the basement, and removed from the job. It was only 60 sheets, but any backwards steps are so much harder than forward movement.

Everyone was discouraged by the apparent slippage, but Project Manager Tom Lucia reassured the crew and lifted spirits by marking this occasion as a systems success. In his quiet way, time and again, Tom would soften the edges, reassure, and coach all of us. The system of logging and cross-checking had worked, even if it hadn't happened with split-second timing. If success is measured by response to unplanned events, then the team had experienced a great victory. John Averill likes to remind me how much we all learned each day. No one had all the answers, so we had to work together to identify the questions, as well as the ways to solve them. Vigilance is an all day, every day, thing.

The Northeast United States is served by several drywall manufacturers based in Canada, New England, and the mid-Atlantic region. For the R.W. Kern Center and the Hitchcock Center for the Environment, we turned to National Gypsum because they were preferred by our installers, and because they are interested in our mission.

Gypsum, the core material in sheetrock, is mined and processed like a cement product, in that it is cooked at the end of its cycle of manufacture. This chemical reaction also releases heat. The board is faced with paper, has adhesive applied to attach the paper, and binders and a dispersant for the gypsum core.

National Gypsum operates out of several plants that service the Northeast region. At its Baltimore facility, the company uses all virgin ground gypsum core, natural lignin as a dispersant, and a plant-based binder. At its Portsmouth,

New Hampshire plant, they include 5 percent recycled sheetrock in the core and a binder that, unfortunately, may contain some residual formaldehyde byproducts.

We would prefer to use recycled products in order to open up the waste stream for product waste recapture. Sol Solem at Wright Builders headed up the procurement process, and was also deeply involved in overseeing the waste streams of both projects. Since each type of waste needs a defined recycling destination, using sheetrock with a recycled content is critical if we want to promote a more sustainable materials chain. (For more on this topic, see "Talking Trash.")

The Living Building Challenge allows manufacturing teams to withhold some details of the manufacturers' product contents as long as the manufacturers certify that those proprietary components are free of Red List chemistry. (See "Chemistry Lessons.") For the Portsmouth drywall product, certification on the held-back percentage was not available to the team because the content was not verifiable. We discovered later that this would become a non-issue. But at the time we did the only thing we could do — we forged ahead and ordered the formaldehyde-free Baltimore product. On the second delivery, we got the correct product, regained our footing and forged ahead.

Almost everyone on the team had heard me repeat the story, now consigned to undocumented legend, of how an entire floor of non-approved sprinkler pipe in Seattle's Bullitt Center had gotten picked at the warehouse, loaded, delivered, and then installed before anybody discovered the problem. It had to come out and be redone. That story always brought out groans but reminded us that we really had to get this right. We weren't the first Living Building team, nor would we be the last, that had to take one step back in order to go two steps forward. We were walking our industry in the right direction.

LEFT:
Seamless panels up to fifty-eight feet long were custom-rolled on-site to avoid any lateral seams.

RIGHT:
Roof edge, roof metal, and Atlantic white cedar move harmoniously around the R.W. Kern Center.

Standing Seamless

A SUPER DUTY PICK-UP TRUCK, TOWING WHAT LOOKED LIKE A GIANT FLYWHEEL ASSEMBLY, BACKED INTO THE R.W. KERN CENTER JOBSITE. THERE WERE MORE than a half-dozen guys milling around watching the truck, looking up at the roof, and at Phil Andrikides, the owner of Florence Roofing. Typical for the late fall season, it was a dark and broody morning, and the roofers were part-way through installing their standing seam metal roofing panels. On the ground, there was a light breeze, but we have come to know that wind and weather thirty feet up atop the R.W. Kern Center can be a different story. Handling forty-foot factory-rolled metal roofing panels can be very dangerous if the wind catches them. They bend and whip and the edges are sharp; they can get away and injure the roofers or, even worse, take flight and be lethal on the ground nearby.

As he got out of his truck, I asked Phil what the morning held in store. He said they had decided to field-roll the longest panels — the ones that spanned up to fifty-nine feet — so that there wouldn't be any seams. Forty feet is the size of the longest factory-formed panels that can be shipped over the road. Besides, they're bendy, unruly, and heavy to handle without lots of human hands until they are bundled, braced, or installed. Hence all the roofers and helpers on-site that day to receive and place them carefully. No surface finish scratches allowed!

The rolling machine, about the size of a backhoe, was gearing up with its small generator and donkey engine beginning to whir. Six men stood ready to receive the panels as they came out folded into "pans." Anyone who has seen a home gutter installation will be familiar with that site-rolling machine. This is similar, but capable of rolling a one-hundred-pound, sixty-foot-long sheet of coated steel.

The roofers carefully stacked and nested the panels in sequence one at a time until they had bundles of twenty panels ready and braced — tipping the scales at about one ton per batch — prepared to be lifted up into place by the crane.

The industry-typical procedure for longer sections of roof is to use multiple panels, concealed fasteners, and a lap seam with sealant at the joint. That approach is fine for factory-rolled panels. But Phil wanted nothing to do with that. "You kidding me?" he said. "I don't want any part of roofing seams under those solar panels." He knew that the roofing chosen for the R.W. Kern Center has at least a seventy-year life, the SunPower 360 photovoltaic panels perhaps forty years or more, and that even the best sealant starts to fade and lose some elasticity in ten years. The roof cavity is filled with twenty-four to fifty-five inches of Class I fire-rated cellulose fiber, so any leaks would create a huge, soggy mess.

OPPOSITE:
R.W. Kern Center roof solar array of one hundred twenty-eight kilowatts, is anchored to the seamless roof panels.

LEFT:
Almost weather tight at the R.W. Kern Center.

ABOVE:
Florence Roofing workers shape the standing seam metal roof panels to be fifty-nine feet and seamless, on site.

While none of this failure would likely occur during Phil's work life, he could see up ahead and around that figurative corner. As a maker, he is equally committed to the immediate and the long-term utility of his work.

Phil's approach reflects his decades of experience working up in the air under difficult and dangerous conditions. It's a preventative and precautionary mindset that focuses on precision and detail. It comes naturally to him as the son of a civil engineer and an accountant.

The bent metal flashing work that now glistens on the R.W. Kern Center roof looks like jewelry. It's exactly the type of artistic technique we see daily in Living Buildings, because the Challenge brings out people's best and most creative work. This level of commitment has a rippling effect on other tradespeople, suppliers, and artisans, who observe, emulate, then inspire the

behavior in their own circles. It brings everyone's best effort forward. What an extraordinary way to work and to live.

Jason Forney from Bruner/Cott Architects said he had never seen site-rolled standing seam panels before. Exceeding the architect's expectations with an improved method has many benefits. It builds confidence in the relationship and reinforces the professionalism and commitment of the building team; it enriches the architect's understanding about how things are made, and how they can be made better; it adds a new measure of skill to the architect's practice. At the R.W. Kern Center, Jason Forney had little cause for worry regarding quality control. We were knitted together in a common quest. The workmanship shines on its own as testimony to a commitment to durability, simplicity, and beauty. For Phil, his very best work was only fitting for this unique building and mission.

OPPOSITE: **Nordic Lam laminated timbers head skyward, fabricated by Bensonwood from New Hampshire.**

RIGHT: **Tom Lucia, R.W. Kern Center project manager for Wright Builders points up, to where the really big sticks are!**

Big Sticks, High Stakes

R.W. KERN CENTER PROJECT MANAGER TOM LUCIA STARTED EACH DAY IN THE DARK MOST OF THE YEAR. IN THE LATE winter of 2015, he would arrive at the Wright Builders office well before 7:00 a.m. muttering to himself and practically speaking in tongues. Something like, "I gotta. I'm gonna figure it out even if it kills me." Few of us knew what was going on behind the scenes.

Tom had been hunched over in his home shop late into most nights during that season, figuring out how to detail the roof trusses and microlam timbers for the eastern portion of the R.W. Kern Center roof. He had to set up for the needed anchors and plates for the myriad compound angles. He had to get the materials ready to order, with an approvals process stretching out ahead.

The absence of conventional parallel lines is part of what makes the R.W. Kern Center roof interesting and inspiring to look at, and expressive of natural form and motion. Horizons and planes come and go, gesturing upward. Surfaces lift and shift. But the building work itself comes down to arranging coded interlocking layers of heavy materials that have to be placed and secured high up in the air, mostly by hand.

This roof section has a kick-up secondary plane in the northeast portion, so each truss had to be custom designed

and sequenced to provide that extending slope. In addition, none of the roof overhangs of this otherwise square form are parallel. They taper in an arresting and engaging way, all leading to challenging but interesting carpentry. Tom later admitted to me, "This was the hardest thing I've ever built."

Architect Christopher Nielsen could provide an elevation for the top point based on electronics and theory, but that could not provide what the carpenters needed. Tom built a three-eighths-inch scale model of the R.W. Kern Center roof about four feet long to find the points needed by the framers, such as wall top plate locations and reinforcing needs. He used strips of scrap pine (wide ones for trusses, narrow scraps for the eleven and three-quarter inch microlam beams used in the overhangs), and hot glue. It looked like a kid's Popsicle stick construction project on steroids.

Because of the compound angles and asymmetrical forms, the exact locations for intersecting members were complicated to configure. "They had to be modeled in a way that could be translated for carpenters' rulers, and also into Portuguese," said Tom with a wide smile, noting the native tongue of many of the framers who would be installing the trusses and timbers.

Tom then prepared his own sequenced CAD section drawings, slicing through the model with his computer,

Timber sections ready to rise into place.

and working his way through all the connection locations needed to make the overhangs secure. The engineers reviewed the approach and offered feedback.

When Tom finished his drawings based on the model, he compared his final top point number with the one Christopher Nielsen had derived from his CAD model, finding a discrepancy of less than one half of an inch. Incredible.

The whole assembly required more detailed work, including custom steel plates and hangers fabricated by Accufab Ironworks in Goshen, Massachusetts. The framing crew was a dedicated and talented group from the southeastern part of the state. Sometimes they would make the two-and-a-half-hour trip each way each day, and other times they would stay over at a rented house in Springfield. Comprised of several Portuguese-speaking nationalities, they worked hard and long, with great precision.

Foreman John Averill picked up some colorful and useful language along the way. One cold day when I tried to sympathize with one of the lead carpenters about the bitter winter weather, he smiled and shook his head. "No, I can always add another sweatshirt, but when it's really hot and I take my last shirt off, that's it. There's nothing else I can do!"

When Canadian pianist Alan Fraser entered the completed building, he stopped in his tracks. "Walking into so many institutional buildings, you can feel how they are heavy and square; how they bear down. They compact you as you enter. The R.W. Kern Center is different. It grounds and lifts at the same time. It is in motion, going somewhere." As an internationally recognized expert in the physical structuring of the hands and how the work of the pianist integrates the whole body into music, Alan was in his element.

That's exactly what architect Christopher Nielsen and the Bruner/Cott team imagined and designed, and what Tom Lucia and John Averill had to figure out how to build. The maker's intent that Christopher folded into the drawings also revealed the underlying ideas that the design principals had initiated, so the purpose was evident.

"There were so many critical connection details and very important structural connections that really could not be drawn that had to be figured out," Tom commented. It became an obsession for others on the team as well, as that spring turned toward summer. Wright Builders Operations Manager Linda Gaudreau remembered, "All I could think of was that old movie *Close Encounters of the Third Kind* with Richard Dreyfuss where he's looking at his mashed potatoes and sees an image. That was Tom trying to figure out the roof; his head and heart were both really in this building."

When asked, Tom said it best himself. "A building of this importance really needs to translate and communicate out into the world," he said. "It's not just that it's healthier and more sustainable. The collaboration shows how much more we can accomplish in doing the work itself. Understanding the mission, in an environment of respect, we have more pride in the project; working people have more desire to be here and so the outcome is that much better. The pride means everything; even the sometimes-grumpy people weren't so grumpy! The owner gets a better product in the end, and that really contributes to the overall success." Purpose, respect, and promise beget pride, which gets us up and going to do our best each day.

For Tom in his shop late at night, or for any tradesperson on any day, this means a fresh opportunity to make a difference.

ABOVE: **Nordic Lam timbers in place at the R.W. Kern Center.**

RIGHT: **A trellis pattern of light when the frame was still open, demonstrating how a combination of small wood members and glue lamination make for a solid and resilient region-based structure.**

The human content of superior work is revealed. Tom said, "If our industry worked like this all the time, collaborating, the results would be so much more beautiful, cost effective, and rewarding for everyone. We need to change the design-construction dynamic to get projects built that are better for the owner, for the workforce, and for the whole world."

The Living Building Challenge creaks and groans like a ship at sea, a huge and beautiful thing in motion, where wood, water, and wind work together with power, respect, and balance. That is the feeling of progress, of moving forward.

Concrete Revealed

MICHAEL FROST PAUSED WHILE
GRINDING THE CONCRETE FLOOR SAMPLE
AND EXCLAIMED, "YOU HAVE SUCH
BEAUTIFUL WARM BROWN SAND HERE!"
He kneeled back down and ground away at the top layer of
cement from a two-foot square concrete floor sample, washed it
down with fresh water, and exposed its core. Then he splashed
more water to wet the sample, wiped it with his worn hands,
and tipped it up to shimmer in the sunlight. We just thought it
was sand. What he could see, and the rest of us came to admire,
was the nearly infinite variety of tiny stone fragments that made
up the sand, all embedded in a warm, brown, granular mass.

This sand is the product of hundreds of thousands of years of
erosion throughout the Connecticut River Valley watershed and
includes rock formation remnants from over 11,000 square miles
of disparate geology. No white coral sand here, nor shale sand as
is found in parts of Vermont. Nothing uniform, but rather a subtle
and varied palette. Color and beauty accumulating over time.
Our sand resources are glacial outwash from the rivers, streams,
and glacial lakes of New England, which contain virtually all
of the minerals and formations that occur in northern New
England — crushed by ice and water then delivered by stream
runoff. Inside the building, we tromp around on a priceless
geological museum. Michael's years of experience as the principal
of Vermont Eco-Floors allowed him to see past the surface.

Most of us think of concrete as a hard-grey monolithic material,
heavy and often brutal, creating a rugged beauty. Mostly, it is
the unsung hero of the building workforce, holding everything
up, or down, depending on the assignment. For flooring, it is
either polished and sealed for the appearance we know at a
big box store, or covered with tile, carpet, or other flooring.

For the exposed concrete floor at the R.W. Kern Center, the
team chose a grinding process that would expose the aggregate
underneath the top skin of cured cement. Concrete is made of
cement, sand, and aggregate stone. The aggregate generally
sinks during cure, so the top layer is mostly sand and cement.
The chosen approach at the R.W. Kern Center required the team
to hand-sprinkle or broadcast more of the aggregate stone on
top of the curing pour while it was beginning to stiffen and set.
The gradually stiffening wet surface was troweled only enough
to sink the stone chunks before it got too hard. Later in the
building process, a huge diamond grinder the size of a riding
mower came onto the floor and ground the surface away until the
stone aggregate and sand were exposed and polished to a shine.

The R.W. Kern Center concrete floor is neither inexpensive
nor common looking. It does not attempt to be a bordered,
bounded, or uniform treatment — such appearances are not
generally replicated in the natural world. The exposed stone is
not laid in a pattern but rather it is quickly scattered by shovel
and hand by workers in tall boots as the cure advances. The

Open, hand-scattered pattern of exposed aggregate concrete floor finish at the R.W. Kern Center's atrium features basalt from a quarry barely one mile from the campus.

tradespeople performing this work at the R.W. Kern Center, from Valley Concrete and Vermont Eco-Floors, know the timing by heart. On the day of our pour, it was getting cold and dark by the time these makers wrapped up their efforts. That meant the finishers would be there late into the night.

This process reflects biomimicry, where human makers study and seek to emulate natural processes. Consider an oyster shell and realize that this mollusk is making porcelain under cold water with no moving parts. In the built environment, materials often take on a life of their own, settling into place according to nature's powerful forces. Think of this material as a mini time capsule, with no list of contents.

As we later watched hour after hour as they ground the final floor, wet-vacuumed the residue, the emerging pattern reflected the arc of the thrown stone, so there were subtle overlapping curves, changes in density, and even blank spaces. It is art, with an organic pattern that reflects the nature of the handwork involved to place it there. Looking closely connects the viewer with the worker and the material in one continuous thread. The print of human intelligence and intent is evident everywhere. The appearance is neither uniform nor predictable, mirroring the character of the plantings and open landscape around the building, which can be seen through the expansive glazing. Less is more, and more varied. From this perspective, we see abundance and diversity, not

ragged inconsistency. Hampshire College leaders were excited by the prospect of a joyous, spontaneous, and free-flowing form result. They completely supported the adventure.

At the nearby Hitchcock Center for the Environment, exposed concrete occurs in several floor areas, most notably in the "ecotone" connector between the two main building forms, or "pavilions." Here, artist Tom Schultz of the EnnisArt team devoted months designing and planning, including days he spent on-site developing and staining a map of the Connecticut River watershed right into the concrete surface. (More on this artful process in "Floor Exercises.")

The first flush water tanks and other components of the rainwater treatment process are located within the Hitchcock Center's ecotone. While visitors walk across the watershed design embedded into the floor and view the intimate and distant landscapes through extensive windows on either side, they are also learning about how the rainwater that falls on the site can be made ready for drinking. Placing these observable functions in the physical link between the project's two pavilions — on top of the very watershed the Hitchcock Center works to protect and explore — literally provides for the experiential wisdom, the mental connection. The treatment of the water and the treatment of the larger water supply go hand in hand, stream by stream, bucket by bucket, drop by drop.

These kinds of floors and finishes cost more than carpet and a little less than wood or tile. It will last the service life of the building. What eventually emerges is not fully controlled, but is rather a surprise to be revealed.

Concrete sealers and consolidators typically utilize fairly nasty and dangerous chemistry, full of volatile compounds. Many have phthalates, a notorious group of chemicals hiding in many products, which are known to cause endocrine system disruption and aggressive forms of prostate cancer among other health concerns. They add pliability, stability, and ease-of-manufacture to materials and are used, for example, as the plasticizing agent in U.S.-made polyvinyl chloride (PVC). In Europe, un-plasticized, phthalate-free PVC is used in architectural windows. Unfortunately, not so in North America and all around the world.

Prosoco Corporation is a mid-sized Lawrence, Kansas-based chemical company specializing in waterproofing coatings and sealers. They first faced the phthalate prohibition under the Living Building Challenge when the Bullitt Center Living Building project team asked for alternatives. Instead of responding defensively or ignoring the inquiry altogether, as other manufacturers did, Prosoco wanted to know more. Why, they queried, were builders and designers interested in non-phthalate products? What was the Living

OPPOSITE, LEFT:
Connecticut River waterway and watershed mapped in the Hitchcock Center ecotone floor, using all nontoxic dyes and sealers.

OPPOSITE, RIGHT:
Detailed column infill at all column bases.

RIGHT:
Staff from Vermont Eco-Floors grind the topping off the atrium concrete floor to reveal the brown sand and basalt aggregate just under the surface.

Building Challenge? The Materials Petal? The Red List? Would a phthalate-free product be commercially viable?

They then began learning all they could, eventually reformulating first their building air and moisture barrier, and then their entire product line to remove the component. They found no loss of product performance, critical for moisture- and vapor-control products with a 100-year anticipated service life in concealed locations. In the process, they established themselves as the industry leader in this product category.

Using this largely nontoxic floor finish was easy to apply, durable, and refreshing. It didn't give off that tell-tale chemical solvent stink. And by this time in the course of both projects, most everyone working on them knew that the material choices we were making helped protect the environment as well as the workforce.

It is impossible to overstate for working people the impact of knowing that big industry and big business are working hard to keep us healthy in the field. That care and ambition is then paid back many times over in workmanship and demeanor on the site.

This inspired industrial shift is a story that keeps asking to be told because its effects are so far-reaching. Removing phthalates while retaining performance creates a safer environment for everyone from the factory workers mixing the initial formulations to the teams applying coats at the site to the nearby workforce to the occupants and visitors of the building itself. We already know a lot about the dangers of these chemicals, as their harmful effects on human health have been well documented. The cautionary principle of the Living Building Challenge says, "Stop now!" We know enough to know better than to build these substances into what we make.

Day in and day out, staff, students, and visitors shuffle, skip, and stroll across the R.W. Kern Center pavilion floor, sometimes lingering, sometimes on a mission. Occasionally, I stop people at random and ask them if they like the floor. Most will pause to look at me, then at the sand, and they get it. On tours, when visitors are looking up at the soaring and inspired space, I ask them to get down on their hands and knees. "This is the history of the Connecticut Valley over a period of 300 million years," I tell them. "Right here in the sand exposed in this concrete!"

Linda's Dad

"MY DAD IS THE ONE ON THE LEFT," SHE SAID, POINTING AT THE OLD PHOTOGRAPH. "HE DIED IN 1971 AT AGE thirty-nine of pancreatic cancer, leaving my mom with us five kids." I was standing in the hallway outside of Operations Manager Linda Gaudreau's office at Wright Builders, and she was showing me a 1960s-era black-and-white photograph of a group of young men gathered around 800-gallon tanks, vats, and other machinery. They were in the chemical mixing area of a large-scale manufacturer of household products sold around the world.

In 2013, forty-five years after her father came to the United States, Linda needed to hire someone to assist with submittal packages. Fate delivered Bobbie. While working side-by-side in the office one day, Linda and Bobbie began trading personal stories and discovered they had an important connection through the chemical manufacturer. The next morning, Linda

brought in the old black-and-white photograph that showed the company's chemical mixing room staff. About 30 years earlier, Bobbie had taken inventory for the chemical purchaser at the factory and these were some of her coworkers. She told Linda how she hated having to go into the plant because the stink was so awful. Bobbie pointed out the Polish man who spoke just a little English, and another man who was the father of her best friend. Standing next to them both was Linda's dad, Nil Gaudreau, whom Bobbie remembered fondly.

Nil Gaudreau immigrated to New England from Canada in 1956 at the age of twenty-four, already with a young son, seeking better opportunities for his family. Like many of his fellow Canadian immigrants, Nil had a tremendous work ethic which he passed on to his family by example. As long as she has been at Wright Builders, Linda has made sure that her work is superior, and that all around her have what they need. No fanfare.

CHEMICAL MIXER   Nil Gaudreau of Easthamp-|mixers, each holding 800 gal-| (News Advertiser Photo)
|ton at one of the five chemical|lons capacity.

OPPOSITE:
After Linda's moving remarks, Bill Kern addresses the construction team, while Hampshire College President Jonathan Lash prepares to speak.

THIS PAGE:
Historic photos of the Easthampton factory where Nil Gaudreau worked.

She agreed to tell her story to the entire R.W. Kern Center project team that had assembled for a pre-completion pizza lunch. Hampshire College President Jonathan Lash was wearing his R.W. Kern Center Team tee shirt under his sport jacket and spoke of his deep admiration and gratitude. College presidents rarely have time to attend gatherings like this, but it was so typical of Lash to take that personal, direct interest, and the workforce really appreciated his presence.

Project Manager Tom Lucia provided a warm, upbeat, and encouraging note for all of us. What struck Lash and others most was Linda's courage to tell this personal story in front of the group. The story leads right to the heart of the purpose of the Living Building Challenge Red List Imperative, and is one of the most important reasons why the Challenge is so meaningful to working people.

Most of the men in that old photograph died very young of cancer. It was part of their way of life. Now, here was Linda at the nexus of finding and vetting nontoxic products for two Living Buildings designed to protect people from such exposures. The connection reached deep and personal for her.

Linda said it best: "It is meaningful for me to work on these Living Building Challenge projects because of the advocacy piece and working toward changing the industry by material vetting for Red List chemicals. This work will create not only a healthier building for its occupants and a healthier work environment for our subcontractors and field staff, but also a safer and better work environment for people in manufacturing. In the future, more of them will be able to work with nontoxic materials."

We raise a glass of precious clean water, in a toxin-free workplace, to Nil Gaudreau, his family, and his coworkers.

Creating Sustainable Buildings That Renew Our World

Talking Trash

Just metals.

CROCKER COMMUNICATIONS HAS A
DEDICATED DUMPSTER TO COLLECT
WASTE METALS IN THEIR CONTRACTORS'
yard. All the bits and pieces of boxes, metal strapping, fittings,
and pipe come back there for recycling. Owner and master
electrician Jamie Crocker said they learned these methods by
separating debris at the R.W. Kern Center and the Hitchcock
Center for the Environment. "It really wasn't that hard; just a shift
in habits," Jamie said. "It's the way we work now." Thanks to the
two Living Buildings on the Hampshire campus, this philosophy
is now built into the way Crocker does business every day.

Along the way Jamie started thinking about his big truck that
he drives around full of tools, most of which don't get used
for days at a time. He thought more about all the fuel he was
using and kept trying to figure out how to change what he
does. Bit by bit, he makes changes. We all make changes.

Americans throw away enough food each day to feed all the
hungry in the world, but what about all that construction
waste? Building products come from ever greater distances,
arriving at job sites cushioned and wrapped for travel in
endless disposable wrapping. Day after day, dumpster boxes
rumble away to landfills, where they add their tare to the
210 million tons of garbage generated in the United States
every year. It's true that almost fifty million tons is now
recycled annually, but there's still a long way to go.

Contractors can get certificates from haulers that guarantee
a certain percentage of the mixed waste load will be recycled
by weight, but that does not suffice for Living Building
Challenge projects. We want to know where the stuff goes
to be repurposed, and what it is eventually made into.

By the end of construction at the R.W. Kern Center, all the wood
waste, including plywood, was making its way to a facility in
Quebec that would chip and process it into strand board for
building sheathing. Andrew Solem at Wright Builders had
spent many weeks in the fall of 2014 researching where we
could send waste. Clean wood waste might seem easy, but is
usually composted, chipped for mulch, or pelletized for fuel.

www.DaveWicklesTrucking.com

ALL TRASH

Separated waste stream creates complexity but also opportunity to market the renewables and achieve highest yield on recycling.

Gypsum

Americans throw away enough food each day to feed all the hungry in the world, but what about all that construction waste?

He worked with a firm in Dedham, Massachusetts to locate end users and arrange logistics for getting sufficient loads put together. We did not want to see the materials converted to wood pellets for burning. Our project's wood waste would be returned back into the material stream just one step down from its original content as a new and useable product that, in its own waste form, would eventually be recyclable again. The same fiber might return to one of our later projects!

Cardboard and paper are not difficult to collect, but there is often a shortage of end uses. One high value usage is as Class I Cellulose insulation, which is manufactured from newsprint and other

RIGHT:
Mixed wood waste
ready for transport for
remanufacturing into
building sheathing.

MIDDLE & OPPOSITE:
Reclaimed red oak creates
a warm natural seating area
at the R.W. Kern Center, and
detail of the same flooring
on the second floor.

70

mixed paper. We chose to use this type of product throughout the R.W. Kern Center, keeping foam products to an absolute minimum.

National Gypsum is one of the top recycled paper users in the United States, and operates three paper mills that use 100 percent waste paper to produce facing paper for its wallboard products. One of the plants, in Portsmouth, New Hampshire, uses 5 percent recycled gypsum for its cores. That's what we want in industry: high-value end uses for recycled materials. (For more on the story of the R.W. Kern Center's gypsum, see "Tale of Two Drywalls.")

Closer to home, Rob Pytko with Dobert Mechanical, responsible for the plumbing, heating, ventilation, and air conditioning at the Hitchcock Center, has his own experience of connecting with sustainability. He lives on a tree farm in Plainfield,

Massachusetts with his family. "We thought at first we would do a straw bale house but ended up with a post and beam frame for our new home, built from our own timber, and we used the waste cuts for the other trim and siding parts. Just trying to minimize our footprint and use what we have," he added.

Although Rob had no prior experience with the Living Building Challenge before coming onto the Hitchcock Center job, the project goals made sense to him. He really liked having his plumbing work exposed. Several times he had offered up piping routes to hide the work and was told, "No, let it show. We like the way it looks." Project Manager Mark Ledwell said of Rob and his coworkers, "They were just awesome plumbers, adjusting the water filtration many times, working to get it right and permittable. And it's all out in the open, to see and to learn from."

In the year prior to starting the R.W. Kern Center project, Project Manager Tom Lucia managed a medical center renovation for Wright Builders. Most of one floor of offices was being repurposed, and twenty-eight recent-vintage solid core birch doors, steel frames, and hardware were destined for the trash. With the help of Assistant Project Manager Ann Ledwell, Tom arranged to have it all pulled out of the project, wrapped for protection, and relocated to a storage unit hoping for a new life.

Fast forward about eight months, and we presented information on the stash and its specifications to the Bruner/Cott team. They did not even blink. All the doors made their second debut at the R.W. Kern Center, filling all the door needs for the project except for a handful of fire-rated steel doors and some decorative natural ash doors.

The light-colored natural birch finish blended with the other lighter woods on the project. Architect Christopher Nielsen had been a bit worried about the array of unmatched wood finishes, but found the end result complementary and successful. At this writing, there are no flush wood doors available that are free of Red List components, so the only Challenge-compliant way to get a new wood door is through a millwork fabricator, at the cost in our projects of about $3000 per opening for door and frame. But the Living Building Challenge allows us to reuse previously installed non-compliant products, since their impact has already been absorbed, and their use diverts landfill waste.

Reclaimed wood floors and stair treads are really the standout trash-to-treasure story at the R.W. Kern Center. Take a moment and time travel back to when Maryland was heavily forested in the seventeenth century and our young oak saplings were getting their start.

More than 150 years later, loggers with hand saws and oxen would fell them and float them downriver to the Chesapeake. There they would be converted into mill timbers for the booming industrial revolution. Those timbers had their second life as the structure of a tannery, demolished in the late-twentieth century. Tom Harris of Architectural Timber and Millwork acquired them, stored them in his inventory of more than three quarters of a million board feet, and converted them to one-inch flooring planks and laminated wood stair treads. The wood we walk on in the R.W. Kern Center was alive and growing in the time of early Williamsburg, Virginia. It's ours not so much to own but ours to use with care, to respect, and to honor… for perhaps another century.

72

ABOVE & NEAR RIGHT: In process, and then two years later, site-salvaged timbers at the Hitchcock Center get new life as benches.

FAR RIGHT: Reused doors from a medical center saved cost and eliminated waste.

Atrium at the R.W. Kern Center.

Jason's Teeth

Jason Jewhurst reviews design materials.

A DOZEN SLENDER THREE-EIGHTHS-INCH DIAMETER POLISHED COPPER REFRIGERANT LINES PROCEEDED OVERHEAD IN THE R.W. KERN CENTER ATRIUM IN perfectly parallel lines across their hangers, turning ninety degrees first right and then left, towards what would become the Kern Kafé area. I had previously sent a note to President Jonathan Lash that there was beautiful jewelry to be seen in these functional parts. He, too, had looked and admired.

"It looks good, but it makes my teeth hurt." Project Architect Jason Jewhurst was looking up at the piping as we walked through the space after a Tuesday project meeting. Startled, I asked what he was seeing. All proper workmanship but Jason was bothered by the fact that the piping was resting on top of clunky hanger bars, which, for him, spoiled the great look of the sweeping, shining copper. The visual here for Jason was like fingernails on a chalk board, a sound that digs deep into the jaw and aches.

RIGHT: **Refrigerant distribution piping at the R.W. Kern Center.**

FAR RIGHT: **Copper refrigerant piping prior to insulation.**

BELOW: **President Jonathan Lash pauses prior to re-hanging and insulation to enjoy the craftsmanship.**

74

The mechanics he asked about the orientation of the hangers commented, "We can use them either above or below. This is just how we did it. But we can change them if you want." After Jason made sure he was not asking for an under-performing application or added cost, they agreed that that particular section of visible hangers would be inverted to allow the pipes to hang free.

Christopher Nielsen reports that the mechanic took it in stride but did step outside for a few minutes to get some fresh air and regroup. Any artisan or tradesperson knows that it is ten times harder to tear apart your own work than to do it in the first place.

Jason came again a few weeks later and noticed that all the visible hanger racks throughout the building had been inverted, to reveal the sweeps of piping. When he inquired, the same mechanic reported, "Yeah, after we talked and changed that one, we thought it really did look better, so we just changed them all." It was

technically unnecessary work, but done willingly anyway. As for the mechanics, altering something to make it look more graceful was refreshing but not unfamiliar. It is a natural thing to do, especially when supported by their boss and the entire team, on their journey together as makers.

Even a maker's story sometimes comes abreast of insurmountable code requirements. That was true here. Those beautiful copper tubes ended up having to be covered with black Armaflex insulation. Since the lines carry refrigerant to deliver heating and cooling supply all around the building and operate in a range of temperatures from 40 to 130 degrees Fahrenheit, they need to be insulated. Otherwise, heat would be wasted into the travel space in winter and cooling would cause condensation to rain down in humid weather. Once they were covered, the piping no longer gleamed like the glint of gold fillings. The beautifully shaped bends and long runs were tucked away in a cozy jacket!

Living Building Makers

Raising the roof at the Hitchcock Center.

Hard-Working Wood

WE HAD JUST LIFTED UP THE INITIAL FIRST-FLOOR WALL PANELS ON THE NORTH SIDE OF THE R.W. KERN CENTER and we were excited to be getting vertical with the mass of the building. Architect Christopher Nielsen came to the Tuesday job meeting, took photos of our wall sections in place, and shared them in his office. The structural engineers and architects looked closely and sounded the alarm: there was too much wood in the walls.

The builders are required to provide the means and methods and are also directed to meet applicable codes. Many designers and builders think buildings are too heavy and getting heavier instead of lighter, more resilient, and less material-intensive. The conflict between a better thermal wall with less framing and a seemingly code-compliant wall with too much wood was resolved by removing some members and retaining others.

Throughout the building process, Mark Ledwell, a co-owner of Wright Builders who served as project manager for the Hitchcock Center for the Environment and a master carpenter in his own right, told the teams that "the rough is the finish." The structure and all materials are visible. As we searched for wood structural elements, we came upon a captivating junk-to-jewels story.

Nordic Lam is a Canadian company that harvests black bog spruce after about seventy years. These are small caliper trees from a cold climate. If one were to take floor joists or other wide stock from this tree, small as it is, the resulting timber would be unstable because of the hard, strong but brittle "pith" at the center of the board. At Nordic Lam, they extract this hard, dense, "junk" core and create a formaldehyde-free waterproof lamination that is as strong as old growth Douglas fir. Each piece is about the size of a furring strip, but together they provide immense strength. Nordic Lam can provide stock for virtually any structural member that can be drawn with pencil or stylus and transported on a truck! Visitors to both of the Living Buildings at Hampshire College love the beauty of the wood, the conservation message, and the "rags to riches" or "splinters to timbers" story.

The Living Building Challenge reminds us to look closer for what we need, where it may be hiding in plain sight.

Moving up to the roof structures, Brian Tetreault, a truss designer at Universal Forest Products in Belchertown, Massachusetts, wanted to fulfill our needs for long-and-strong wood trusses for both the R.W. Kern Center and the Hitchcock Center for the Environment. But he needed 2000 PSI spruce, not the ubiquitous 600 PSI framing material that is readily available in the East. Vermont-based r.k. MILES Building Materials Supplier located a source in Eastern Canada, virtually in our backyard. The Living Building Challenge reminds us to look closer for what we need, where it may be hiding in plain sight.

The Hitchcock Center budget could not support laminated timber or reclaimed timber for the roof structure. After a few days of puzzling, architect Sam Batchelor suggested doubling up standard trusses for a nominal four-inch member so that they could be spaced twice as far apart for a much more spacious, open feel. Once again, Brian Tetreault's team stepped up, using the high strength eastern spruce. Universal Forest Products made these doubled-up trusses in sets of two, so that the indelible lumber markings printed on one side of the sticks would be concealed.

Early in the R.W. Kern Center planning, architect Jason Jewhurst asked me, "What do we have for finish woods to use on the exterior?" The old standbys of redwood, cypress and red cedar are geographically too distant to meet the Challenge's local sourcing requirements. There was only one answer to this multiple-choice

Living Building Makers

RIGHT:
Mitered microlam wood structure to carry the unsupported cantilever.

BELOW:
R.W. Kern Center siding pre-stained and ready to go aloft.

LEFT: Even the wood chips have a higher calling, here delivered for initial stocking of the composting toilets.

TOP: R.W. Kern Center foreman John Averill prepares the laminated stair treads for their inset steel wear bars.

ABOVE: Timbers for both buildings are a Nordic Lam glue-up of small black spruce cores.

Creating Sustainable Buildings That Renew Our World

78

Multiple trussed planes of the R.W. Kern Center being assembled slowly but surely.

question. Both the R.W. Kern Center and the Hitchcock Center use Eastern White cedar, a handsome wood from smaller trees in a harsh Northeast climate. It does not have the same levels of natural tannin for preservation, but is weather resistant nonetheless.

Architect Bruce Coldham had tipped us off very early in the process that the Roy O. Martin Company in Lexington, Louisiana had compliant quality products. As construction progressed, we had used a full tractor-trailer of plywood but now we needed an additional partial trailer to finish the projects.

Joe Miles and his team stepped right up. They had already relocated their FSC designation to our local branch yard to support our Living Building needs.

Their operation has four lumber yards in several states. In Massachusetts, carpenters prefer fir plywood, but in Northern Vermont they prefer the southern pine product. In order to fill the Roy O. Martin truck hitting the road from Louisiana, Miles bought many extra forty-four sheet units of pine plywood to fill out the load. They then shipped this extra stock to their yard in Middlebury, Vermont, where the carpenters like it.

Why have craftspeople, builders, and artisans down through the ages been drawn to wood, this endlessly varied living material? The heady wood and leaf smells of New England trees and forests remind us of home. Trees spend their lives taking in carbon dioxide and discharging oxygen, which allows humans to continue breathing. Trees are keeping us alive. And after we cut them, they help us become makers of beautiful, durable, resilient, and useful things.

Creating Sustainable Buildings That Renew Our World

The Best
I Can Do

ON A CHILLY LATE-WINTER MORNING
AT THE R.W. KERN CENTER, I FOUND
BOB KUDA, A LONG-TIME SHEET METAL
technician — or "tin knocker" as he's known in the trades — up
on a ladder securing the last of four exposed assemblies of twelve-
inch round spiral heating and cooling ducts. The ducts emerged
through a wall from air handlers and other gear in the utility room
over to the right, then traveled overhead above the Admissions
Center hallway, before heading out into the atrium area.

"It's the best I can do," Bob said, responding with shrugged
shoulders to my compliments about this manifold of ductwork
that looked like the supercharger pipes on a *Great Gatsby*
roadster. I realized that Bob was sort of apologizing for the
duct seam sealant mastic that he had applied. This sticky goo,
almost the consistency of pine pitch, is usually slopped on
and hidden like so many other trade work details. But here, it
was exposed. The ductwork itself was not planned for paint,
so its mill-finish would remain. Nothing would be hidden.

Bob told me his boss discouraged him from using masking tape, so
instead he had used small sticks and his fingers to work the putty
into a fairly uniform ring of sealant. "It took a while to figure out
what we were trying to do here on this job," he said to me over
his shoulder, "but now I think it's coming out pretty great."

The pattern of the cylinder's undulating path overhead was
undeniably beautiful. The movement of these pipes out through
one wall and in through another was almost anatomical and
reflected the intended work of moving fresh, clean air.

Then I saw, through the door opening out across the upper
atrium, Bob's counterpart, the sheetrocker, working on his quiet
answer. Patiently, he was scribing and cutting the drywall to
fit. Actually, he was using scraps to make templates so that he
could fit the drywall precisely to the metal work. While these
ducts are considered cylindrical, their actual shapes are affected
by shipping, drops, dents, and handling. The sheetrocker was
on his third pattern scrap for this particular cut, working to get

OPPOSITE & LEFT:
Hand-assembled
custom ductwork
exposed to show the
craftsmanship and
the function.

BELOW:
Exacting drywall fit
and finish highlights
intersections of
different materials.

the slightly uneven radius just right. He could tell that the sheet metal work was superb, and this was now his go-to standard.

Sheet metal workers and drywallers almost never see each other because the rough ductwork is usually installed by the time the drywallers come on the job and the drywaller's typical assignment is to cover everything up. But in Living Buildings, with the admonition of "no unnecessary finishes," all the working parts show, and all of the markings of the workings shows as well. Here again, the words of Wright Builders' Mark Ledwell resonate: "The rough is the finish."

Work in the building trades, often carried out in dirty, poorly lit, and cramped locations, can be repetitive and sometimes oppressive. When it is transformed by design into an expression of craftsmanship, beauty is revealed. At the R.W. Kern Center, the best that one "tin knocker" could do was more than enough to add startling elegance and grace.

Creating Sustainable Buildings That Renew Our World

Peter touches up the mortar on the south wall of the R.W. Kern Center.

Peter and the Schist

WATCHING MASON PETRO ("PETER") NEPEYVODA
WORK, ARCHITECT JASON JEWHURST REMARKED,
"I WONDER HOW HE WILL HANDLE THE CORNERS."
It was a matter of interest and curiosity, not supervision or concern. I told Jason
I didn't know either (yet), but to come back in a couple of weeks and see Peter's work,
as it usually spoke for itself. Jason was content. I began to mull how, indeed, the corners
would be woven with this irregular material.

Peter is a compact, alert man with a weathered face. Sometimes, in cool weather,
he trades in his sweatshirt for a handwoven sarape for additional warmth. Peter is
always in motion, always working. He is working when examining the stone one
piece at a time, when chipping stone, when mixing mortar for stone. Peter is working
when he is standing still.

While Peter was busy laying up veneer at the R.W. Kern Center and approaching the
first exterior corner of the building, Jason came on-site for one of his occasional visits.
While Bruner/Cott's Christopher Nielsen handled much of the day to day architects'
work, Jason always had a big-picture overview, and I looked forward to his insights.

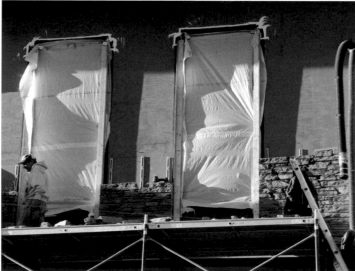

ABOVE:
Schist weathering
in, or leaching out,
over a long winter.

FAR LEFT:
R.W. Kern Center
veneer in process,
showing the
stainless-steel
anchor system and
the Prosoco Cat 5 air
vapor barrier.

LEFT:
R.W. Kern Center
south side stone
veneer complete,
ready for windows.

FAR LEFT:
Turning the corner with seamless grace and ease.

LEFT:
Schist window sills.

BELOW:
The Kern Kafé counters are also polished Ashfield schist echoing the stone wall behind.

The traditional industry hierarchy that places architects over builders remains pretty standard. But more and more, and especially — essentially — on Living Building projects, the whole process must be a collaboration. In the particular case of stone masonry for the R.W. Kern Center, we, as builders, were charged with finding the right people. Unlike when laying brick or cut stone blocks, the plan for laying irregular split schist is not something that can be drawn on a computer.

For weeks, the team from Vladimir Bondar Masonry had been preparing to lay up this veneer on the building's face. Vlad was the boss but Peter, a former mechanical engineer from Ukraine, was the most expert. Vlad's brother-in-law, Vassily, also helped out.

Over 100 tons of stone segments lay weathering to the west of the building site. A balance of colors, sizes, and shapes; of order without pattern or inadvertent trends like sagging course lines. One stone at a time was picked up from a small pile near the staging area, and chipped into final shape by hand. The buildings' courses and corners rose step by step, as naturally as if the stone had been literally folded around to the adjoining façade.

On his next visit, Jason stood back and marveled. I asked him, "Can you write a specification for that?" He shook his head and grinned. We had made something more than a thing: we had introduced inspiration to this building; this project; this campus. Peter and Vlad and the team had transformed stone into beauty with their bare hands.

Ashfield schist sitting wall manages grade change while creating a sense of place and a moment to pause.

Early on, when the building team suggested the possibility of utilizing local schist for the building veneer, architect Jason Jewhurst made a twenty-mile trip to visit Johanna Pratt at the Ashfield Stone Company quarry and nearby workshop. (Wright Builders has a decades-long relationship with the Pratt family and its stone products.) Jason liked what he saw and established a good rapport with the Pratts. Not surprising, as Jason comes from a background of masons and carpenters, so he has an affinity for the place and the work. It is part of his DNA as a maker.

The stone formation on the east slope of the Berkshire Hills in Western Massachusetts continues northward to southern Vermont. Its geologic life dates from approximately 404 million years ago, making it by far the oldest and most venerable material we used at either the R.W. Kern Center or the Hitchcock Center for the Environment. Iron ore for steel, limestone for cement, and basalt for aggregate are all much younger geologic neophytes. Its name, "schist," derives from the Greek "to split" because it is metamorphosed from a layered sedimentary formation, originating as lake bottom, and separates relatively easily at the layers. For years, this schist has been used largely as patio and landscape wall stone, generically known in its more southerly and slightly softer forms as "Goshen stone."

In the 1990s, the Pratts developed the capacity to quarry, mill, and polish the local stone in countertop-size panels in the hilltop shop in Hawley, Massachusetts where they lived at the time. They also devised how to quarry the erratic boulders and other irregular parts of the formation to reveal astonishingly varied and beautiful artisan stone. One finds embedded crimson spots, the start of garnet formation, and a host of other striking colors and details in virtually every piece harvested from these veins of schist, both at the quarry and around the region.

The Pratts had recently made a major investment in a new building and equipment to saw and polish larger panels, while improving the quarry equipment to make snap stone. In this

It took Peter and Vlad more than four months to hand-lay this endlessly irregular material into a rich, dignified kaleidoscope that functioned as a fully weatherproof building exterior.

latter process, slabs of quarried stone, such as those used for patios, are surface-scored and then snapped with a hydraulic machine to produce a four-inch veneer stone. That was our stone.

It took Peter and Vlad more than four months to hand-lay this endlessly irregular material into a rich, dignified kaleidoscope that functioned as a fully weatherproof building exterior. For the small rural quarry, the order provided a valuable boost in sales and visibility by showcasing this new application of very old rock in a signature building. Something local, unusual, innovative, beautiful and full of story was, literally, a perfect fit.

Back when Peter had laid up the first lower sections of the schist, applying a veneer over exposed concrete foundations, everyone admired the look. Then it rained. The stone began to bleed oxides, with rust-orange color cascading down the face of it. We washed and sealed, washed and sealed. I had nightmares about the gorgeous R.W. Kern Center beginning to take on the appearance of a beached and rust-streaked freighter. What would we do? We carried on and held our breath. As it turned out, where the stone was not in contact with concrete, there was no bleed. More washing, sealing, and waiting. Even

when the rains came again, all was well and no one quite knows why. Innovation has its fiercely anxious moments.

The team saw every reason to expand on its usage elsewhere in the R.W. Kern Center once the sourcing was accomplished. Indeed, so many advantages and efficiencies accrue in doing so. (Just because one uses garlic in the ceviche appetizer, does that mean no garlic in the pesto?) Repeated uses of the same core materials in different applications is expansive, helping to create connection and continuity among different forms and spaces within a building. Regional cuisines and Living Buildings are like that.

All the window sills in the R.W. Kern Center are half-inch-thick polished Ashfield schist, handsomely offsetting the black aluminum window frames and the gleam of the glass. The Kern Kafé counters and Admissions Center reception desktops are also a thicker, polished schist. The tile wainscot caps in the bathrooms are milled from schist.

Outside, abutting the south entrance patio, there is a sitting wall section made of the same stone. Large stone chunks are arranged as seating for an outdoor classroom and gathering space just to the east, visible from inside the Admissions Center waiting area. These seating stones were provided by the quarry in exchange for returned extra veneer snap stone. How else but through local sourcing could all of that happen?

In the early fall of 2015, I again told Peter how beautiful his stonework looked. His face lit up in a very restrained way, and he said, "Jon, three or four more days, we will finish, and then I will never see you again." I was struck by the mix of his deep pride in his work, the unique experience of his work with this stone, and his sadness in leaving. All around the building, other tradespeople knew what good stone work looks like, and this was among the very best they had ever seen. All of us, aware or not, followed the rhythm of his patient focus and determination as it folded in with precision and art.

A few weeks later, Peter was back with us on another Wright Builders project, laying up concrete block for an elevator shaft.

The wildflower meadow lays claim to the the building,
as the natural balance settles into place.

Finished R.W. Kern Center southeast face, also showing informal stone chunk seating.

He was engaged in everyday work that doesn't get much attention. But I now knew him as a maker at the R.W. Kern Center, the project that brought out the best in all of us. Peter later returned to Ukraine for personal reasons, but we will never forget him.

For the trades, our work is how we say thank you. The Kern family knows how to say thank you in their own way. Bill Kern, especially, as a photographer and film artist, felt the impact of all of our work and re-confirmed his determination to have a thank-you event for all the trades when the project was completed. Bill wanted all the makers to bring their children and families to a celebration to share what they had done. When Lee Kern, Bill's mother and Ralph Kern's widow, was planning the occasion, catering staff offered her various plate options starting at fifteen dollars per person. She said in her endlessly generous way, "Fifteen dollars? What do I get for FIFTY dollars?" It was indeed a splendid barbecue of burgers, dogs, ribs, chicken, sausages, vegetables, towering salads, multiple sides, desserts, beer, and wine. Everything. And of course, Lee's signature request for all occasions: chicken salad, light on the mayonnaise.

Gratitude is a feast, for the body and the soul.

Floor Exercises

Living Building Makers

WHEN WE WALK INTO THE ECOTONE CONNECTOR BETWEEN THE TWO LARGER PAVILIONS AT THE HITCHCOCK CENTER for the Environment, we know exactly where we are in the world. We are walking through the Connecticut River watershed. The deep water is rich blue, the shoals are sandy colored, and the swamps are a deep green — all rich tones with lively color texture. It is at once understated yet loud and clear. When I first saw the finished product, I wanted to get down on the floor and crawl the beautifully detailed river and Connecticut Valley watershed map stained and etched into the concrete floor.

Fine artist Tom Schulz and his artist nephew, Daniel de Wit, spent months planning and days carefully mapping the details of the twists, turns, meanders, and oxbows of the river. Architect Sam Batchelor had brought them in for this commission. The work is exacting and permanent. No delete key strokes and "tracked changes" here.

The Living Building Challenge gave Tom and Daniel the push, imperative, and guidance to find healthy, vibrant alternatives. "Now we have a complete line of stains available from Prosoco that are not only phthalate-free, but also free of all volatile organic compounds," Tom excitedly reported to me. "These materials and the Living Building Challenge completely changed the way we work and what we offer to our clients."

Back in the 1980s when Tom transformed his Tufts University MFA into this design specialty, the methods were basically acid etching and stains, which were toxic and caustic. For years he chased and handled solvent-based products and myriad polymer stains. All that is changed now, thanks to the innovation and leadership from a company in Lawrence, Kansas which itself has transformed its entire product line. (For more on Prosoco products, see "Minds and Hands in the Gutter," "Concrete Revealed," and "Battling the Bulge.")

I caught up with Tom just after he and Daniel had returned from installing a labyrinth design and six-foot Tree of Life for a church in, of all places, Lawrence, Kansas.

"There is so much anger in our country now with poorer working people feeling disenfranchised, feeling that no one listens to them and their plight. The Living Building Challenge answers that in a small but important way, through advocating for healthier products," said Tom. Back in 2011, when the Bullitt Center in Seattle went in search of phthalate-free products, Prosoco famously began reconfiguring everything it makes to be phthalate-free.

As they work all over the country, Tom and Daniel can work all day on the floor, bent over this rainbow of rich color options, painting and staining as if they were using watercolors on paper.

Battling the Bulge

THE CONNECTICUT VALLEY WAS ABOUT AS SULTRY AS IT CAN GET. SUMMER 2015 HAD FINALLY ARRIVED, STRAWBERRIES had ripened, and the weather was going nuts. Temperatures heaved up into the nineties with comparable humidity. Overnight fog hung low, and afternoon thundershowers made it feel more like the Gulf Coast than New England.

One soggy morning, R.W. Kern Center Foreman John Averill had his four-foot-long level in hand to check some layouts against the north wall studs on the first floor. He checked and tipped the level to plumb, and then looked again, confirming what he saw the first time: the wall was tipped out nearly one and one-quarter inches. Weeks of wet while the complex roof system was assembled had taken its toll on the laminated wood decking of the second floor. The wood and glue were fine but, despite all efforts, the decking had sucked up

OPPOSITE:
The second-floor
expansion shows at
the upper part of
the sheathing corner.

RIGHT:
Bit by bit, the
building is pulled
back to dimension
after cutting out a
length of planking.

the residual rain and atmospheric water from the swampy conditions and the constant parade of afternoon downpours.

The moisture content of wood makes it change mass. After all, swelling oak pegs driven into bore holes were used as the method of choice for breaking up granite in quarries. The wood wants what it wants, and will get it. These scientific realities were playing out right under our noses, and feet, at the R.W. Kern Center.

John reconfirmed that the second floor in the east wing had, indeed, grown before ringing the alarm bells. Let's just say some calls were made. He and Project Manager Tom Lucia seemed focused and calm, but I was doing somersaults inside. We were all on edge. The structural engineer on the architects' team, once informed, issued a stop work order, without much other guidance. The College, however, did not tell us to stop. No other letters were sent; no postures were struck.

Project Manager Kerry Uhler from Bensonwood in New Hampshire, along with their foreman CJ Brehio and their in-house structural engineer, brought forward a method to repair and document. "This happens pretty often when wood decks are not provided with room to expand and contract and pick up moisture due to environmental conditions," Kerry explained. They proposed to cut out a strip, pull the building back together with chain and cable comealongs, realign a few posts, and put a replacement smaller splicing strip back into the floor. Their own structural engineer devised the system and stamped it with his professional license.

The underlying worry was whether the modified floor system would retain its ability to perform all of its duties. The answer was yes, thanks to the resilience and adaptability of wood. The near-miracle of the wood roof assembly process is discussed elsewhere. (See "Minds and Hands in the Gutter.")

ABOVE:
The R.W. Kern Center is prepared for its roof structure and weeks of complex carpentry.

NEAR RIGHT:
Laminated black spruce second-floor deck planking at the R.W. Kern Center.

FAR RIGHT:
Slowly closing the gap after planking was removed.

Along the way, the integrity of the project team was strong enough that the repair could be made without a major unrepairable rift in the project.

Behind the scenes, Carl Weber from Hampshire College quietly contacted the Construction Technology people at the University of Massachusetts, where the study and promotion of wood for structural uses goes back to the University's origins as Massachusetts Agricultural College. Alex Schreyer, director of the Building and Construction Technology Program at the University and an internationally recognized author and structural engineer, visited, inspected, and also confirmed that the event was not entirely out of the ordinary.

He commented that we had used shiplap laminated planking with the grain all in a single direction, rather than cross-laminated-timber, or CLT, which would have significantly retarded the expansion process. He tested the wood, and determined that once repaired, that floor would be stable and sound.

John Averill and his team repaired the sheathing, touched up the moisture barrier coating, and put the matter behind them. Mostly. We always remember the close calls, and how solutions are arrived at by working closely together. We are all members of the herd of elephants in the room who never forget.

Along the way, the integrity of the project team was strong enough that the repair could be made without a major unrepairable rift in the project. Resilient organizational design is natural and based on trust. The forgiving properties of wood and the creative power of the practitioners who rely on it have an unmistakable affinity.

Chemistry Lessons

ANDREW "SOL" SOLEM, USUALLY PATIENT
AND UNFLAPPABLE, WAS GETTING FRUSTRATED
AND WORN OUT FROM THE LACK OF PROGRESS.
The short, frayed end of his rope was in sight. Two months and no answers. We had
thought the Red List compliance information would be forthcoming from the major
manufacturer we had selected for the electrical equipment for the R.W. Kern Center.
But, like many companies guarding their manufacturing and business processes,
representatives from this one were reluctant to disclose their components or to
formally certify that the undisclosed items were Red List-free. Finally, Sol, Lisa
Carey Moore from Integrated Eco Strategy, and Project Manager Tom Lucia had had
enough of the head banging. It was time to start over with a different approach.

Conduit clips reveal a puzzle about
materials toxicity. The answer is classified.

Following a stint working the Midwest after graduating from the University of Massachusetts, Sol made contact with classmate Richie Frend who was working on materials vetting at Wright Builders. He soon joined the effort.

It was a curious job assignment to start with — a mixture of site labor along with materials and waste management. The work also included site administration, request for information (RFI) logs, submittal status, and other reports. I didn't quite see how it would all work, but Tom Lucia and my partner at Wright Builders, Mark Ledwell, were convinced it would.

Then Sol gradually and reluctantly gave up his time in the field and came inside to oversee the daunting process of vetting materials. Mark had come upon Sol simultaneously using three computers and gliding back and forth effortlessly among them — and realized what capacities this guy had.

By the time Sol made his way down the project's materials list to the electrical equipment, he had transformed into a savvy materials researcher. The day had come. There was no turning back — we needed electrical switch gear NOW — a message that was always packaged in his deceptive mildness.

OPPOSITE, LEFT: Securing Red List materials confirmation of the R.W. Kern Center transformer took more than two months. All of us were new to the process.

OPPOSITE, RIGHT: Transformer at the Hitchcock Center was researched and approved in two weeks.

LEFT: Inverters take the R.W. Kern Center direct current solar panel output and convert it to alternating current for building use, shedding some heat into the basement in the process. Handy for winter comfort and humidity control.

BELOW: Moving power and communications around the R.W. Kern Center through nearly five miles of beautifully shaped and placed conduit.

Everything changed with a phone call to Square D, an Andover, Massachusetts-based electrical equipment manufacturer, part of Schneider Electric.

Square D was eager not only to disclose its formulations, but to become an active participant in our efforts. With their help and accessibility, Sol was quickly able to advance the long list of equipment for review and vetting. We did all our buying for both Living Building projects from Square D via Crocker Communications, our electrical contractor.

Reduction of Hazardous Substances (RoHS) is the European electrical standard, adopted as a benchmark by the Living Building Challenge. It is known in the trades by how its acronym sounds — "Rowhouse." It turned out that Square D was already well on its way in making a mammoth voluntary shift in its entire product line to achieve 100 percent RoHS compliance. As the projects advanced, Sol was able to query any product in their line and determine whether it was RoHS-

make and do, and have come to expect in the developed world, extracts its human and environmental price. The search for nontoxic products makes for a tough assignment, but one that our team's owners, designers, and contractors embraced. It is a race against the poisoning of the earth.

Instead of seeking work-arounds and waivers for materials on these two projects, we needed a way to organize our research and streamline our manufacturer outreach processes. The help we sought from Integrated Eco Strategy proved invaluable. Charley Stevenson, Kath McKusker, Don Mulhern, Lisa Carey Moore, and their team had previously completed one Living Building Challenge project in our region. They provided the methodology, research, contacts, and third-party record keeping of the research and results. They were ready when the project teams called, supporting Sol's leadership and dogged efforts on both buildings.

> Materials supply is a jungle. Can we build with materials that support the community, provide jobs, and heal rather than exacerbate centuries of injustice? Most of what we make and do, and have come to expect in the developed world, extracts its human and environmental price. The search for nontoxic products makes for a tough assignment, but one that our team's owners, designers, and contractors embraced. It is a race against the poisoning of the earth.

compatible and, if not, when that would be achieved. This supplier was completely and happily transparent.

By the time the Hitchcock Center for the Environment began purchasing, the process was clean and practiced. Electrical contractor Jamie Crocker had worked with his supplier to upload only the Challenge-approved products into the order database accessed by electricians in the field. They could not order anything delivered to the job that was not compliant. Still, order-picking at the warehouse is not foolproof, and most orders contained items that had to be returned once site staff performed quick database checks on their phones. Delivery drivers sometimes grew frustrated, but the process worked, thanks in large part to the diligence of field electrical foreman Barnaby Young and his team.

Materials supply is a jungle. Can we build with materials that support the community, provide jobs, and heal rather than exacerbate centuries of injustice? Most of what we make and do, and have come to

We had leverage. Not a long lever, but one we could bear down on. The combined 26,000 square feet of new construction in these two projects gave us new negotiating power through volume with manufacturers and suppliers. We rediscovered the obvious: that project size means dollars, which means attention and opportunity for the industry.

The Living Building Challenge asks teams to follow the "precautionary principle." The Red List of highly suspect chemicals and classes of chemicals have been identified and are being augmented with each new version of the Living Building Challenge. It does not make for easy reading because it is dense and full of long chemical compound words, often misspelled in industry. (See Sidebar) But it's all part of helping create a less toxic built environment in which the simple act of breathing will be safe and restorative.

Even as the inventory of Red List chemicals and ingredients grows, the data on approved project materials far outpaces that growth, making Living Buildings easier and more efficient to create. Each new Living Building Challenge project adds information to the total known catalog.

On reflection, using fewer materials in a building and fewer components in a product makes life simpler, the process plausible, and the results prone to fewer errors. (See "Peter and the Schist" for more on multiple uses for stone.) For example, there are only perhaps a half dozen light fixture types in the R.W. Kern Center, and none of them has more than seven components. With fewer coatings and ingredients, teams can get to the bottom of the components and chemistry with greater certainty. All the while, fewer products are being used, creating less process waste.

While the Red List is not exhaustive, it covers some of our industry's worst public health and environmental offenders, whose various compounds and permutations show up in thousands of product ingredients. The Red List provides an aperture through which to see how our persistent cultural appetite for more products and ever greater convenience has disregarded the impacts of the products' components on people, natural systems, and health. As purchasing volumes increase and awareness grows among manufacturers regarding the toxic consequences of these materials to the workforce, the Living Building process is making huge progress. It is getting easier and what a breath of fresh air it is.

Living Building Challenge materials vetting charged into 2018 with a breakthrough. A nationwide database developed from actual project materials lists, called Red2Green, was launched by Integrated Eco Strategy and born of their materials research for eight Living Buildings. Following the completion of the Hitchcock Center and the R.W. Kern Center, Integrated Eco Strategy continued to work on more Living Building projects, gathering an impressive storehouse of materials information.

Overseeing the materials that make up the two Living Buildings standing on the Hampshire College campus fundamentally changed Andrew Solem, and he left his mark on the process as well. To this day, subcontractors express their deep gratitude when they say again and again, "Sol, I just could NOT have done this without you."

MATERIALS RED LIST

The R.W. Kern Center and the Hitchcock Center were registered under Version 2.1 of the Living Building Challenge, whose Red List was comprised of the following materials:

Asbestos

Cadmium

Chlorinated Polyethylene (CPE)

Chlorosulfonated Polyethylene (CSPE)

Chlorofluorocarbons (CFCs)

Chloroprene (Neoprene)

Formaldehyde (added)

Halogenated Flame Retardants

Hydrochlorofluorocarbons (HCFCs)

Lead

Mercury

Petrochemical Fertilizers and Pesticides

Phthalates

Polyvinyl Chloride (PVC)

Wood treatments containing Creosote, Arsenic, or Pentachlorophenol

Volatile Organic Compounds (VOCs)

Pizza and its documentation, hand-carried as hot-list item to architects in time for lunch.

Pizza and Beer

DESIGNER CHRISTOPHER NIELSEN WAS BENT OVER HIS DESK AT BRUNER/COTT ARCHITECTS, FOCUSED ON YET ANOTHER INCOMING MATERIALS SUBMITTAL FROM Wright Builders for the R.W. Kern Center, oblivious to what was afoot. Week after week, the relentless parade of packages explaining the sourcing and composition of each material being used in the building would arrive, often referencing a sample to arrive under separate cover. Over a span of nearly two years, more than 800 products and materials would run this course, as compared to perhaps 150 in a typical job of this size. For each weekly conference call, the "Hot List" was reviewed, comprised of items tightly time-constrained and needed on the job.

On this day, Sara Draper in the Bruner/Cott office seemed very keen on one incoming submittal. Just before noon, the "hot" item arrived: a fifteen-inch pizza, complete with the proper Living Building Challenge documentation and content analysis for the food and the box. Sara had been conspiring with Andrew Solem, her counterpart at Wright Builders, to arrange receipt of this special lunchtime submittal.

The submittal was very thorough, using all the proper forms and tracking information developed over months of materials vetting. Each product submittal comes with a Material Safety Data Sheet, or MSDS. In this case the MSDS read, in part:

Jason Jewhurst and Christopher Nielsen at Bruner/Cott carefully review critical data on the pizza submittal from Wright Builders. Christopher pens an urgent comment on murky cheese sourcing, quickly snapping a picture before all the evidence is gone.

Disclaimer: The information contained on the Material Safety Data Sheet has been compiled from data considered to be absolutely inaccurate. This data is believed to be completely unreliable; it must be pointed out that values noted for certain product properties are also not true. All vendors presented in this Material Safety Data Sheet are made up and by no means relate to any company that actually exists. Therefore, the maker of this Material Safety Data Sheet assumes no liability for any injury or loss arising from the use of this product. It is the responsibility of the reader to understand this and not overreact. There are no federal or state regulations on products that do not exist. The actual pizza may be hot, so the entity creating this Material Safety Data Sheet assumes no liability over any injuries pertaining to the pizza delivered. Remember to recycle.

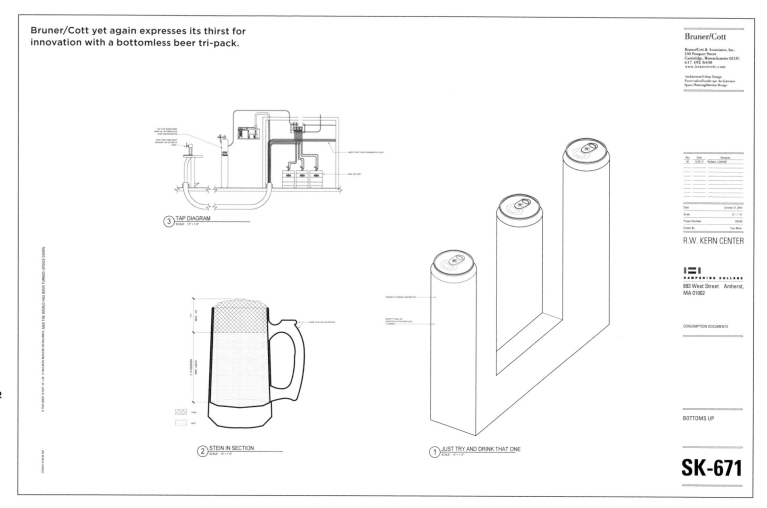

Bruner/Cott yet again expresses its thirst for innovation with a bottomless beer tri-pack.

③ TAP DIAGRAM
SCALE 12" = 1'-0"

② STEIN IN SECTION
SCALE 12" = 1'-0"

① JUST TRY AND DRINK THAT ONE
SCALE 12" = 1'-0"

Bruner/Cott

Bruner/Cott & Associates, Inc.
130 Prospect Street
Cambridge, Massachusetts 02136
617 492 8400
www.brunercott.com

Architecture/Urban Design
Preservation/Landscape Architecture
Space Planning/Interior Design

R.W. KERN CENTER

HAMPSHIRE COLLEGE
893 West Street   Amherst,
MA 01002

CONSUMPTION DOCUMENTS

BOTTOMS UP

SK-671

The pie was met with instant approval and was marked "revise and resubmit" before it disappeared. Was it the pepperoni, the cheese, the sauce, or the crust? The evidence had been consumed. Architect Jason Jewhurst joined in the fun, with everyone finding welcome relief from the taxing research and vetting of materials.

The pizza submittal also raises a side (salad?) bar question: What do we really know about what we eat? Did the team perhaps just stumble upon the root stock for the Living Food Challenge, which at the time had not been broached? But I digress...

The following spring, the Wright Builders team was alerted to an important bulletin coming in. Bulletins are clarifications, changes, or new instructions for the contractor, supplanting or adjusting the original design documents. Contractors work to abide by the bid documents, including specifications, addenda, and big rolls of drawings as well as endless catalogs of emails and online record keeping. The documents often contain inconsistencies — they are prepared by human beings, after all. Clarifications and additional instructions, along with sketches and other updates, come in the form of sequence-numbered bulletins.

It was among Christopher's jobs to draft bulletins for the Wright Builders team, to capture any changes and keep the job moving and up-to-date. That spring day, we were told to expect a delivery to the Wright Builders office at 4:00 p.m., and we were asked not to leave without receiving the package. A pleasant but stern directive.

Meanwhile, back in Cambridge, Bruner/Cott folks were scrambling to track down a mailing tube at least three inches in diameter and thirty inches long to ship the bulletin — it had to be just big enough to hold six twelve-ounce cans of beer — along with a shipper willing to carry out such a delicate, custom-critical and precise assignment!

The Beer Bulletin was born, and arrived just before quitting time on Friday, accompanied by a full specification section #067100 "Beverages" from the standard CONSUMPTION DOCUMENTS. The architects provided full details on storage, use of openers, types of suitable glassware, and so it went:

Glassware: Provide serving vessel as noted:

1. *DEEP, TULIP-SHAPED GLASS - Strong beers, such as Belgian ales*
2. *SIMPLE PINT GLASS - Mild ales and brown ales, porters, stouts*
3. *SMALL, BRANDY SNIFTER–TYPE GLASS OR CORDIAL - Rich and spirituous barleywines, old ales, and imperial stouts*
4. *THIN, STEMMED FLUTE - Some Aromatic Trappist and Abbey Ales and Belgian Fruit Beers*
5. *TALL, NARROW GLASS - Light, spritzy, and aromatic beers, such as Pilsners and witbiers*
6. *TALL, THICK GLASS - Wheat Beers*
7. *WIDE-BOWLED GOBLET - Aromatic beers, such as Berliner Weisse*
8. *RED SOLO CUP - Bro beers such as Natty Light and Pabst Blue Ribbon, or any beers mentioned in country and western-style music*

LBC Submittals: LBC Documentation: Submit a completed Section 018111 — LIVING BUILDING CHALLENGE (LBC) SUBMITTAL FORM for each product required. Particular attention should be made to sourcing requirements. Site visits to manufacturing facilities may be required.

Bulletins are clarifications, changes, or new instructions for the contractor, supplanting or adjusting the original design documents. Contractors work to abide by the bid documents, including specifications, addenda, and big rolls of drawings as well as endless catalogs of emails and online record keeping. The documents often contain inconsistencies — they are prepared by human beings, after all.

The accompanying sketch under the title "Bottoms Up" includes a unique impossible-object design for a three-topped beer can. It is not always easy to get a handle on the architect's design intent, particularly on a Friday afternoon at 4:00, and particularly while holding a warm beer. Fermented beverages were developed by early communities because the lack of sanitation made drinking water unsafe. The relaxing effect and probiotic contribution make these excellent for humans.

Which brings us back to the Living Building Challenge, where net zero water usage is an Imperative. Given the number of naturalists, educators, and biologists in circulation around the R.W. Kern Center and the Hitchcock Center for the Environment, both of which collect and retain far more water than they need, the Living Brewing Co. might not be far off.

Water Music Suite

PART I: HOPE IS PERMITTED

Architect Jason Jewhurst and civil engineer Chris Chamberland were on a call one morning with the Massachusetts Department of Environmental Protection (DEP). They were inquiring if and how rainfall could be harvested and stored on-site for drinking water usage at the R.W. Kern Center. Not just to make the water safe, but to elevate it to public water supply standards while keeping it chlorine-free. (Similar proposals had been presented a few years earlier on behalf of Smith College's Bechtel Environmental Classroom, later certified as the fourth Living Building.)

The expected answer was no again but quickly the conversation turned interesting. Cisterns are illegal for public drinking water in Massachusetts, after so many decades of striving to overcome compromised private water supplies and replacing them with safe public drinking water. Fetid backyard or basement tanks come to mind.

Something different was afoot. The DEP engineer said, "Well, you could use the standard form of application for a municipal public water supply reservoir, Form WS-15." It had been years since a public water reservoir had been built in Massachusetts, but the application process was still in place. He continued, "When you get to the lines about watershed catchment area size, just cross out 'square miles' and put in 'square feet.' On the line for storage capacity, just cross out 'acre-feet' and write in 'gallons.'" Getting to "yes."

Be careful what you wish for. Now the path forward was infinitely more challenging and interesting, as compared to a flat "no," which would have had the projects connected to municipal drinking water with a Living Building Challenge "waiver."

The storage vessels for roof-harvested water would henceforth be called reservoirs, never mind that they look remarkably like cisterns. It was clear that the Living Building Challenge had sparked the interest of yet another part of the design and construction world: water permitting and public health.

Courtesy of Peter Vanderwarker

Full array of piping for both rooftop collection planes for rainwater at the Hitchcock Center passes through the ecotone connector, where students and visitors can watch, marvel, and learn.

OPPOSITE:
Sections of the R.W. Kern Center's reservoirs are carefully lowered into place by the staff of Karl's Site Work.

Word had gotten out through the rumor mill in Amherst about what we were proposing. It is a small community with agriculture roots and knowledge-culture roots, so town boards are well stocked with really knowledgeable people. They did not have to allow us to pursue site-treated water at all. But their message was: "If you can get state approval, we will support you." It is part of the culture of the town to foster innovation and curiosity. Pride of accomplishment follows closely behind.

At the very beginning of the design phase for the R.W. Kern Center, the team met with all the town officials to present plans for the project. Each permitting jurisdiction within town government had their comments and suggestions. Town Engineer Guilford Mooring's request was simple and direct. He wanted our water system and its processing located in the basement, and the town water service for fire suppression up on the main floor. "It has to be set up so that no matter what happens, if every back-flow preventer fails, power fails, everything is compromised, earthquake, whatever, there is NO WAY that potentially site-contaminated water from the building systems can find its way into the municipal supply,"

Guilford said. His message was simple and clear. The system had to be 100 percent secure, and the team made sure of it.

During construction, Jay Klemyk and the other tradespeople from Karl's Sitework had painstakingly assembled the precast sections of the "reservoirs" with the required sealants and gaskets. Later, they would open the locked stainless-steel access lid and climb down inside to apply waterproofing to the inside. The coating had to be suitable for drinking water, free of Red List chemicals, but durable enough to keep acidic rainwater from leaching the lime out of the concrete. Acid rain literally eats cement.

The Hitchcock Center for the Environment was moving along in parallel. Some of our staff said that the Hitchcock Center was drafting the R.W. Kern Center. Yes, reduced headwinds! But plenty of paddling through water issues lay ahead.

Nevertheless, the collected water would need treatment and filtration. Maybe we had the permitting in the bag, or in the tank, but some real fun was about to start.

PART II: SEEKING TREATMENT

At the design kickoff for the R.W. Kern Center, Jason Jewhurst from Bruner/Cott Architects asked, "Who's going to design the water system?" Without taking a breath, Rick Klein of Berkshire Design said, "We will." Rick was a principal and landscape architect at Berkshire Design until his death in 2017, and an amazingly creative, bright, and productive force. Often, he was the lead on projects that required his firm to deliver both landscape design and civil engineering services. At the R.W. Kern Center, his firm handled the civil engineering and he was the partner in charge because of his role as the College's site planner and his extensive credentials.

Taking over the water treatment as a civil engineering role, even though it was to be housed entirely inside the building, meant that all of the water treatment functions would be integrated. Over in the other corner of the room, I saw mechanical engineer Jim Lewis sigh and almost smile. He was relieved to be handing this assignment to Rick's team.

Chris Chamberland was brand new to the civil engineering team at Berkshire Design at that time. It's the beginning of a

As the time to connect the systems approached, Hampshire's project manager and mechanical engineer Todd Holland wanted to really know the condition of the water in the reservoirs. After all, it had sat untreated for many months. I had wondered the whole time if we would find a green slimy sludge when we finally took a look!

He opened the hatch and could see clear to the bottom 10 feet down. He was so excited that he tied his cell phone to a string and lowered it into the tank to get pictures and video... of what nothing at all looks like. On this particular day, what "good" looked like was as clear as a mountain stream. Neither the images nor the cell phone survived, but the story remains.

What is it about the water system that keeps the water so clear, even after months of storage? First, the rainwater has never hit the ground, been a nursery for beavers and fish, crossed a highway, or sat in a swamp. The first gushes of water driven off the roof and through the downspouts by gravity activate the turbine "WUSY" filters, using just the hydraulic pressure of the water itself, which then throws off most of the debris

> # He opened the hatch and could see clear to the bottom 10 feet down. He was so excited that he tied his cell phone to a string and lowered it into the tank to get pictures and video... of what nothing at all looks like.

very special story, because Chris got under the weight of this water system like a stevedore. Mild-mannered, patient, funny, and very sharp are some of the traits we admire in Chris.

The potable water treatment area and greywater treatment area in the R.W. Kern Center basement are like two small seminar rooms, open to the basement hallway separated by a low wall and a chain across the door opening as required. Here groups can gather for training, inspection, and informal small group discussion.

FAR LEFT: Greywater effluent at the R.W. Kern Center finds its way to these planters, nourishing the foliage, adding healthy humidity to the air, and expressing a seamless relationship between water and plant materials inside and outside the building.

NEAR LEFT: Sara Draper, R.W. Kern Center Director of Education and Outreach, does her basement chores which include checking the coffee grounds that build up in the greywater system.

BELOW, LEFT: The truth does not hide. Greywater always dresses in purple.

BELOW: Planters fed by greywater provide a calming influence to offset the excellent coffee!

into the waiting bioswale. The next one-eighth inch of rainfall is called the "first flush," and that cleans the roof of other dirt and debris such as bird droppings. Roof water is diverted into the reservoir only after the first flush tank is filled. All of this happens with gravity, without any electrical parts.

On the R.W. Kern Center job one day, plumber Patrick O'Connor and his boss, Jim Moran from M. J. Moran Mechanical Contractors, were with us checking out the basement water treatment area. The usual process of submittals and corrections for the water treatment system had advanced quite far.

After a bit of conversation, Patrick said, "Why don't we just assemble the parts of the system, with all the filters,

TOP LEFT:
R.W. Kern Center water treatment system, as updated and simplified over the course of the first year of operations.

BOTTOM LEFT:
The Hitchcock water treatment system differs in detail but uses many of the same components.

Creating Sustainable Buildings That Renew Our World

Architect Sam Batchelor mocked up the Hitchcock water collection system nicknamed "Sebastian."

These tradespeople were eager to figure it out and make interesting stuff that works and endures. What a great way to work, and what a great thing for the College, and the design team, to allow. A less controlled process governed not by jurisdiction and authority, but by thought and skill and trust, makes people thrive.

shutoffs, etcetera, as we think it should work, and would be easy to maintain, referring to the drawings of course?" The architects looked skeptical. Nobody EVER offers to do the work and then modify it for free, just to make sure it works best. Jim added, "We'll redo it in any way you want, make any changes afterward, but we just think, since the concept is brand new, if we mock it up everyone will get to see what works and how it could be improved."

Meanwhile, at the Hitchcock Center for the Environment, architect Sam Batchelor envisioned the first flush tank as transparent and located inside the building where everyone could see and hear the treatment process. Out of curiosity, he built a

half-size mock-up of the first flush system and attached it to the roof downspout at his home. Nicknaming the test device Sebastian (which his young children found hilarious), he reports jumping up from the dinner table more than once to check on it when a downpour began.

These tradespeople were eager to figure it out and make interesting stuff that works and endures. What a great way to work, and what a great thing for the College, and the design team, to allow. A less controlled process governed not by jurisdiction and authority, but by thought and skill and trust, makes people thrive.

It won't be long before a comparable package system can be ordered, pre-approved, with the click of a few computer keys.

The simple life of clear water and its shimmering molecules ends here at the inlet valve, as the drops and cups and gallons make their way through the basement treatment area to become a new substance: chlorine-free potable water, courtesy of the Massachusetts Department of Environmental Protection.

PART III: RICH AND FAMOUS

"You know, I think those boys have been in the bathroom a little too long," remarked Colleen Kelly, education director at the Hitchcock Center for the Environment during a project team reunion held after the Center had been open for more than a year. "Usually that means they are writing on the walls with the Clivis soap, or popping the soap bubbles in the toilet bowl," she said with a wide grin.

These Clivis Multrum composting toilets use a tiny amount of water and soap to aid the flush through four-inch piping, instead of the twelve-inch straight drops used in the R.W. Kern Center. A faint hum announces that bubbles are initiated, before and after use. This is endlessly fascinating, especially for young ones, and even more so when the curriculum at the Hitchcock Center draws attention to the waterless waste

system. Colleen takes it all in stride, even when her six-year-old granddaughter comes home from Hitchcock Center visits excited that she knows exactly where Grandma's poo goes.

There seem to be two groups of visitors to the two Living Buildings on the Hampshire College campus — those who would prefer not to think too much about the big black composters, and those who can't wait to look inside. Mostly the latter! Lift the lower bin lid and there is a mix of wood shavings, peat moss, and liquid, from which the excess blackwater is pumped to tanks as needed. This concentrated nutrient-rich wastewater still has to be disposed of at a wastewater treatment plant. But soon, Hampshire students and faculty will collaborate with the Hitchcock Center to study, test, and propose a way. That's how they think.

Water is the elixir of life and the life of the party for young people in summer at the Hitchcock Center.

As for the "famous" part of our tale, word spread like spilled coffee. People were curious — especially when it came to dead silent and unfamiliar toilets. When I tell visitors that as many as 600 people enter the R.W. Kern Center every day, and total water usage is only around 120 gallons, they are startled. I am told Williams College students go out of their way to use the composters in their Living Building Challenge Petal-certified Class of 1966 Environmental Center. These fixtures are cool, fun, and strangely quiet. There is no bowl water!

Hampshire Microbiology Professor Jason Tor even suggested he might raise funds if they could be called Tor-lets. He's excited because the microorganisms are in charge and doing a great job of cleaning up after us. And none of that waste material is being flushed, pumped, treated, settled, chlorinated for river discharge, or trucked to landfills.

With weekly maintenance check-ins and further additions of chips and peat moss, the waste solids and paper decompose. After a couple of years, there will be a wheelbarrow or two of humus to remove and bury, destined once again to become soil, from which all food comes. It takes time to get that rich nutrient, when the volume reduction is in excess of 95 percent, about the same percentage reduction of maple sap to maple syrup!

Flush toilets would require as much as 1500 gallons a day of fresh water for each of these Living Buildings, which could not be supplied by the rainwater systems. When we look at the whole system, radical usage reduction is the only path to capture nutrients, spare the waterways, conserve drinking water, and recharge the groundwater.

The composters vent constantly so there is never any odor and, initially, the waste air went through the energy recovery ventilation system to recapture the heat. Over time, we had another uh-oh moment when winter winds started to back-feed those fumes into the fresh air intakes. The inlet and outlet were properly separated, but the combination of wind patterns around the building, and the pungency of the compost and blackwater exhaust venting were not a good mix. Unlike the dairy solids waste from the Kern Kafé (See "Four Scientists Walk into a Diner"), this was more of a dairy farm flavor, a little sweet and cloying as well as, well, all the rest of it.

ABOVE, LEFT: **Jessica Schultz of the Hitchcock Center morphed her Capital Projects Coordinator role into becoming the master, and master teacher, of systems at the Center. Here she does a light seasonal raking!**

ABOVE: **Sara Draper freshens up the wood shavings and peat moss of the R.W. Kern Center composters.**

OPPOSITE: **When all reservoirs are full at the R.W. Kern Center, which is often, the extra water wends its way through the bioswales to a constructed wetland, shown here with flourishing wildflowers at its border.**

PART IV: JUST THE WEATHER

This is a quiet story. Shhhh. The only sound is the trickle and occasional rush of pure water. There are no humans, cell phones, or exclamations. Just water and soil. It takes about two inches of rain to fill the reservoirs at the R.W. Kern Center and the Hitchcock Center for the Environment, which, in turn, is a ninety-day supply of water ready for treatment. The Western Massachusetts region enjoys about forty-four inches of rainfall per year and is getting wetter, so there is lots of excess to be returned to the soil and groundwater. Where does it go?

Like lightning, water goes to ground. No moving parts, just the great engine of regeneration. Overflow from the WUSY filters, designed to separate and discharge solid materials and debris, spills out on the ground. The slow drip of the first flush tanks finds its way to soil. And once the reservoirs fill, all of the rainwater goes onto the ground. Chris Chamberland and Karl's Sitework reappear in our story, engineering and constructing the bioswales that collect, spread, and direct and disperse the water. Constructed wetlands and ponds are ready for stormwater overflow. The whole concept is to keep the water, nutrients, and topsoil right here so it can enrich this place rather than travel out to sea.

Grasses, shrubs, and stones slow the water down, helping it to take its time. What's the hurry really? Let the ideas and the water just soak in.

Reclaimed and laminated Appalachian red oak, here adorned with one of the R.W. Kern Center's intriguing puzzles, are finished with Polywhey from Vermont Natural Coatings.

Varnished and Untarnished

PAINTERS WERE VARNISHING WOODWORK IN THE BIG, OPEN TWO-STORY PAVILION AT THE CORE OF THE R.W. KERN CENTER. ABOUT FIFTEEN FEET AWAY, a young pipefitter was preparing fittings. "What do you smell from the painter over there?" I asked as I ambled over. He looked up and said, "Oh, I didn't know he was applying the finish. Is there a problem?" "No, not at all," I said. "That's a really good urethane wood finish made in Vermont from dairy whey waste, and it does not stink!"

The young man looked startled, as if he had been expecting a reprimand, then pleasantly surprised by the direction of our chat. He grinned broadly, put down his tools for a moment, went over and picked up the can and took a sniff. He shook his head, smiling, and went back to work saying, "That's cool!"

When I first asked Nordic Structures, the Canadian manufacturer of Nordic Lam timbers, about how to finish the product we had ordered for the R.W. Kern Center, their representative, Jean-Marc Dubois, immediately directed us to Vermont Natural Coatings in Hardwick, Vermont, population 3010. My first thought was, "Is this stuff really any good?" Cost concerns and shipping considerations also popped into my head, given what I assumed was a tiny operation headquartered in a tiny town. I love Vermont, but my professional bias was definitely showing.

I discovered that Vermont Natural Coatings products have been stocked in our two major lumber yards in Western Massachusetts for years; we just never knew to ask for them! They are low in volatile organic compounds (VOCs), including petroleum by-products, which harm their makers and users. Vermont Natural Coatings poly chemistry uses the whey by-products of the northern Vermont regional dairy industry. It is easy to apply, levels well, cleans up easily, dries predictably, and does not give off a chemical odor.

The professional painters love it: it's durable, comes in all sorts of formulations, and is easy to get. Pat Coffey, the painting contractor for both Living Building projects on the Hampshire campus, said, "I'm using this stuff from now on. No stink and it lays down really well too." Two years later, Pat reported he was still using it nearly exclusively not only for its chemistry, but also because it is simply better to work with green products that protect the workforce and perform better.

As it turns out, Vermont Natural Coatings is one of several small manufacturers based in Hardwick, Vermont. The small town has been reinventing itself for the last twenty years as a sustainable food community, even with

its short growing season and rocky soils, and is known for its great cheeses, meats, and prepared foods.

Here's how Vermont Natural Coatings' founder, Andrew Meyer, tells the story:

"We manufacture our products in my hometown of Hardwick, Vermont, where my family operates an organic dairy farm. I started Vermont Natural Coatings from a conviction that the choices we make about materials used in our homes, schools, and workplaces should include consideration for health and the environment. We've grown by building strong relationships with store owners, contractors, and homeowners. Each connection is based on providing the very best wood protection, while making application and living conditions dramatically better."

Once again, the Living Building Challenge required us to seek and secure a better way to do what we do. As a result, our buildings are cleaner, their makers and occupants are healthier, and a regional business gets a boost. Everybody wins.

I have witnessed what I hope is the last generation of professional painters and other tradespeople, many of them my friends, who have succumbed to disease and alcoholism that can be traced to solvent exposure. While many of today's products have come a long way, most still include mildew retardants composed of chlorine derivatives and other formulations that bring unknown long-term consequences. New health and environmental dangers follow on the old. The newer products may be good, but they're not all benign.

I'm so grateful we listened to the advice given by our Canadian colleagues who offered up this ideal and change-making local solution. Once again, the Living Building Challenge required us to seek and secure a better way to do what we do. As a result, our buildings are cleaner, their makers and occupants are healthier, and a regional business gets a boost. Everybody wins.

116

Gathering in a circle of connection, continuity, and change at the new Hitchcock Center for the Environment.

Habitat Exchange

THE HITCHCOCK CENTER FOR THE ENVIRONMENT STAFF AND FRIENDS SET OUT ON THEIR THREE-MILE MIGRATION TO THEIR NEW HOME ON THE HAMPSHIRE College campus in August 2016, following the tracks of native toads and salamanders, and mimicking the long treks of aboriginal inhabitants, and also travelers everywhere. They walked next to the ditch along West Street with water bottles, bundles, and packs. What a journey they had been on to get to this moment, this transition between building and inhabiting.

Two years earlier, back in the design phase, Education Director Colleen Kelly had said, "We were so comfy in our old home, even piled on top of each other. We loved the smells, the trace odor of skunks, and it was hard to imagine how a new building could be warm and friendly like this." But the old building shouted out its shortcomings and its weariness, finally bidding them farewell and safe travels, doors and eyelids sagging. The time had come, and habitat exchange was underway. It was much more than replication; it was a new universe under the same sky.

LEFT: **Hitchcock friends and family make the three-mile long migration to their new home.**

OPPOSITE, LEFT: **Part of making friends, and making friends with a new place, is making something there, together. Something useful and important.**

OPPOSITE, RIGHT: **Ancient trees on the site provided an opening through which to see into the future.**

Matt Kirchman, principal at ObjectIDEA, brought his video and museum education experience to the project, which helped define goals during the early planning phase. He collaborated from the beginning with the staff and the design team. As the Hitchcock Center staff worked to describe their vision for the two outdoor spaces they hoped to incorporate into the new building, Matt listened carefully and then offered his interpretation: "One is a nest; the other a den." Bingo. The areas were not named "southeast" or "northwest," but called by the feelings they conveyed and the function they would fill for generations of learners.

After the staff had been in the new space for a while, we reconnected as a group to share stories. It was a wonderful opportunity for me to learn more about how the Hitchcock Center's education work had changed since transitioning into their new quarters. As we talked, the staff dug into their light supper and perked right up. "I would like us to have our own collection of stories on our dashboard that people could also connect into," Colleen remarked. "Because the feel of this place, this wooden building is so good! I was fearful of a modernized glassy looking new energy-efficient building," Colleen commented.

> "The Living Building Challenge and our new building just took us to a whole different level of thinking and teaching about sustainability; it is so completely empowering for us."
>
> JULIE JOHNSON,
> HITCHCOCK CENTER EXECUTIVE DIRECTOR

Hitchcock Center Executive Director Julie Johnson fills any room she enters with her conviction, her combined sense of playfulness and urgency, and — at six feet tall — her stature. "The Living Building Challenge and our new building just took us to a whole different level of thinking and teaching about sustainability; it is so completely empowering for us," she said. But it had been a long process getting to moving day.

Julie reflected on the feelings the building elicits in its occupants. "I came to realize that the project was not just about us having a beautiful solar building," she said. "What's become more important to me is that it reflects health and wellness. And

somehow, this place does still feel cozy and warm even with exposed mechanical systems and more office-type fixtures."

They had all committed very early to the Living Building Challenge. Hitchcock Center folks do not mince words or mission. But who knew what that transformation would really look and feel like? At our story-sharing gathering, Children, Youth and Family Programs Coordinator Katie Koerten reported, "The sense of ownership that has happened as a result of being here comes from our intimate relationship with the building. We all have it as a result of what this building does. In my experience, our caretaking is so different in terms of how we relate to this physical structure because it's almost a living creature." As Katie sees it, the building has taken on a life of its own.

These educators are so immersed in their work and in identifying teachable moments that their own learning is likewise transparent and agile. When the building began to talk to them, they could listen. The wood and glass have a soul that speaks, albeit quietly.

Students, teachers, and visitors derive more than a sense of wellness and health inside the Hitchcock Center. They actually experience it, thanks to the construction itself. "Knowing it's a healthy building and that these materials

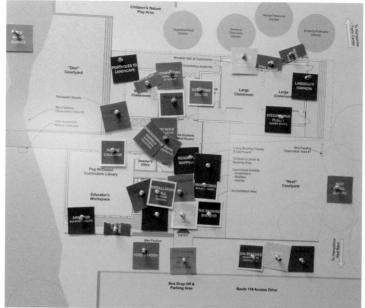

> "When people come to visit, they have this emotional connection with the place that goes beyond anything I can describe."

MARCUS SIMON, HITCHCOCK CENTER
DEVELOPMENT COORDINATOR

aren't toxic to us gives me a feeling of safety," Colleen added. Cozy was good but wellness and safety — these are strong values coming out from, well, the woodwork!

What is it in the architecture, the materials, the building work itself that carries this caretaking message? The stewardship mantra? School Programs Coordinator Helen Ann Sephton bantered a bit with her colleagues on this subject. "For me, the beams are the saving grace. While I appreciate the soft white stain on the walls because it's light and it's cheerful, it's the beams and their color tone and the exposure of the structure that makes it cozy." "And all the little knots!" offered another staff member from across the room.

Colleen has a way of coming back to the big picture. What brought her around to really embracing the building during construction and move-in was specific. "Even after we had gone through all the green building details, what hit me was that this building, a Living Building, was going to be such a forward-thinking educational tool." Julie added, "When I thought about how much hopefulness would be right here, that made me feel very grateful. This building empowers me and my own work as director." Hope is a treasure to seek and cherish.

Julie continued, "We have young interns coming from all the area colleges to Hitchcock to work. They tell me stories about the things they are learning in class and how depressed they were that the world was falling apart and that there were no solutions. Being here gives them energy and focus. That's what I mean when the hopefulness hit me." When a building tells you that things might just be okay, and offers you its companionship and reassures you that it will help you achieve your goals, it's a powerful call.

Development Director Rebecca Neimark said it another way. "I like how everything is exposed so I can see all the details of the structure. I see all the tubing. I feel it's a transparent building, just as the staff here are really transparent with each other."

OPPOSITE, LEFT:
Detailed hands-on planning processes at the Hitchcock Center helped the architects and staff focus on the needs and aspirations, as well as desired project characteristics, leading to beautiful and child-friendly functions.

OPPOSITE, RIGHT:
Hitchcock trustees, committee members, and staff all played key roles in shaping the project.

LEFT:
Hitchcock Executive Director Julie Johnson teaching, presenting, leading.

I don't think that is a coincidence. The building has its own transparency, because you can see it and see right through it, and that is equivalent to how we deal with each other; how we relate to each other, and to our students and the community."

The Hitchcock Center's Communications and Living Building Coordinator Jessica Schultz remarked, "Long-time friends of the Center, once perhaps skeptical of all the newness, now come in and say, 'You know, it feels a lot like that old Center.' I think it does have that rustic feel to it, with the wood. There's something that did translate with this place. There is a certain scale to the building and the windows and especially the connection to the outdoors that we didn't really have until now, that amplify that sense of continuity." Jessica has now reinvented herself as the building's guide, keeper, and knowledge bank. She can be found almost any day checking filters, fielding press inquiries, arranging and providing tours, and keeping an eye on the roof drains, among many other duties.

Colleen added, "People are unexpectedly surprised at the power of the place and what it does. A lot of people just are not even aware. They just are coming cold. And it really blows them away."

Perhaps unique for this team and this building is how that translates directly to moving the staff from inhabitants to makers. Exchanging habitats is about preservation and renewal. Hitchcock folks make and remake their Living Building story every day.

"When people come to visit, they have this emotional connection with the place that goes beyond anything I can describe," reflects Development Coordinator Marcus Simon. "Being here and feeling it is something that we can't package up, but it is so real. We took these big theoretical concepts and made it happen. People talk about what we should be able to do, or need to be able to do to not completely ruin the world. While it seems so incredibly difficult to achieve, it is possible. We did it!"

Inside Out, Outside In

PROFESSOR ALEJANDO CUELLAR SOFTLY CLOSED THE DOOR TO ROOM 202 ON THE SECOND FLOOR OF THE R.W. KERN CENTER. Something about his gentle manner made me stop him in mid-stride across the loft gallery and ask him how he was using the room for his teaching.

"I teach a creative non-fiction course called 'The Space in Our Identity: Writing About Home' in this room each week," he said. "It's mostly first-year students working on their writing skills."

He told me, "At first, I was a little concerned about all the glass and windows. Maybe it would be distracting." As the semester got underway, he found the opposite to be true: "Actually, the room seemed to relax the students."

It's biophilia at work. The presence of outside experienced on the inside, the balance of natural and manufactured materials, the evident and reassuring structure, and access to the visual and sensory resources of the natural world all play a part.

Room 202 contains a reclaimed wood floor, two solid interior walls, and two exterior walls of glass. The wood-bearing posts are visible at the perimeter, the substantial glazing frames are not too far apart, and the windows feature several operable sashes. In other words, occupants experience a sense of solidity and openness all at once. The room provides a kinetic place to learn and to be creative. "The space in our identity" indeed.

I shared this report with Professor Christina Cianfrani, who also teaches in that room. Her official field is hydrology but she teaches a broad range of topics. She looked at me, very kindly, as if I had just noticed the sky was blue.

"Oh, yes, it's a great place to teach. We study rainfall and water issues, and every time it rains, we just look out the window and watch the rain gardens, stormwater constructions, and wetlands do their work." For her students, the natural world within reach just outside the room's windows provides the same baseline of openness and containment as it does for the writers in Professor Cuellar's workshop, with the huge added benefit of having a peekaboo observation lab that doesn't require putting on a raincoat.

What is more like home than opening a window to listen to the rain, after all?

On rainy days at the Hitchcock Center for the Environment, just one thousand feet away, Wright Builders Foreman Jim Small, on a post-construction visit, came to see rainfall in a whole new way after his year building the structure. "It's not precipitation. I can hear the rain come and go in intensity. What I hear on the roof is rainwater harvesting; drinking water being made. I can hear the process and the purpose out loud."

Every visitor during a rain event can hear the water come down through the interior roof drains into the glass connector between the two pavilions of the center, called the ecotone. There, two drains take the water, spin it through the centrifugal filter called a WUSY filter to remove debris, separate off the first one-eighth inch of rain into first flush tanks, and then divert the balance into underground reservoirs. Any overflow heads out into a bioswale to feed the Hampshire College farm grazing pasture below.

Coming in the front door of the Hitchcock Center, the water treatment is right up ahead through the glass doors. If the weather has been dry for weeks, the semi-transparent first flush tanks may have residue dust and pollen showing on the inside, which provide learning opportunities.

All through the Hitchcock Center, the natural world is present and adjacent. Most of what the visitor sees is natural materials or the natural world beyond the windows. That is, of course, the Hitchcock Center's mission, and the building itself provides a unique biophilic teaching tool.

124

Making Beautiful, Durable Connections

"THESE ANIMALS ARE VERY SMALL, AND WE WANT
TO TREAT THEM WITH RESPECT," PATRICK O'ROARK
EXPLAINED TO HIS EAGER YOUNG AUDIENCE. THEN
moments later, he circled back, informally reminding, "We treat all animals
with respect and kindness, like we do our friends and our pets."

Patrick had collected early spring pond creatures and vegetation in dishpans and placed
them on low tables around the classroom at the Hitchcock Center for the Environment.
As the Hitchcock Center's environmental educator and live animal caretaker, he had
prepared for a Saturday Family Science workshop for a group of young children and their
parents. He was showing the children how to use a spoon and the scope dish from an
observascope, a small, low-power microscope-like device, to pick up the little creatures.

On this bright March Saturday morning, eighteen months after the Hitchcock Center Living Building had opened, the Center was also introducing its extended outdoor trail and activities plan, which would include a mud kitchen!

It was my first opportunity to observe one of Patrick's workshop sessions in the new Hitchcock Center. And it didn't take long for me to realize that the session was exactly what the building was designed and made for. Adults and children alike were excitedly peering at the small creatures and early spring vegetation that are native to the area ponds, to be repeated in thousands of different ways over decades to come.

How this building was built and its pieces connected is in plain view. Almost nothing is wrapped in sheetrock or hidden except for a few partitions.

Patrick was making the explicit connections for everyone in the room, from the toddlers participating in the front to the octogenarians watching from the back. Core values were coming to life in the murky waters of the dishpans! Discovering how creatures, plants, and natural places interact reveals how we are connected to one another and is a lifelong adventure that starts very early at the Hitchcock Center. Kindness and respect are built into Living Buildings; both are foundational messages of the Hitchcock Center and all it represents.

That same day, right across the hall from where Patrick held his workshop, I made my own study of the Hitchcock Center's elegant exposed connections while listening to a presentation about upcoming site improvements. I should know the connections well, having worked on the project for nearly four years. Yet on that Saturday, I had been away from close contact with the Hitchcock Center and otherwise occupied for more than a year. Luckily, Patrick brought it all back into focus for me!

How this building was built and its pieces connected is in plain view. Almost nothing is wrapped in sheetrock or hidden except

FAR LEFT: **Overhang structure with distinctive, bold joinery exposed at the Hitchcock Center.**

LEFT; **Post build-out from the wall allows for seamless transit of conduit, while steel angle clip eliminates the need for pressure treated wood to anchor the wall to the foundation.**

OPPOSITE, LEFT: **Architectural Timber and Millwork fabricated and assembled the simple but elegant angled beam seats, using Nordic Lam timbers, at the Hitchcock Center.**

OPPOSITE, RIGHT: **Overhang support piers and footings are all fully thermally isolated from the interior structure by rigid insulation.**

for a few partitions. The roof trusses, ganged up in pairs and made from a high grade of spruce from Eastern Canada (see "Hard-Working Wood"), are structural members typically buried in the attic. Here, they are in plain sight, with their bits of bark remnant, knots, and steel press plates holding them together.

The Nordic Lam posts and beams for the walls were planed smooth one additional time (over and above the two provided by the manufacturer for exposed "architectural grade" timber work), and carefully finished by the fabricators at Architectural Timber and Millwork with Vermont Natural Coatings Polywhey. Where a beam comes in to rest against a post, there is a back-cut seat angled in — an elegant, simple, and indestructible connection.

I admired all this while drifting away for a moment from the presentation and the slides. I realized that this connection was like all the others in its mission of respect and kindness.

Pressure-treated wood is required by code for all wood in contact with concrete, to help resist rot and insect infestations. But treated wood is just that, crammed full of toxic preservatives. How to avoid using it? The timber framers and design team opted for post bases that hold the wood off the concrete, so no treated wood was required.

The outside walls were more challenging. In the Hitchcock Center building, the wall assembly is made up of layers applied to the outside of the posts, starting with a spruce tongue and groove plank. I had assumed, grudgingly, that we would have to secure the planks to the concrete by way of a treated wood shoe as we usually do. Then we would also have had to cover it, to protect young visitors.

But Sam Batchelor had a different thought — why not hold the wood up off the concrete by a half-inch and fill the joint

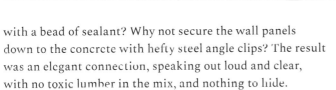

with a bead of sealant? Why not secure the wall panels down to the concrete with hefty steel angle clips? The result was an elegant connection, speaking out loud and clear, with no toxic lumber in the mix, and nothing to hide.

The post back-spacers serve as another connection innovation. Since the wall planking was to be directly applied to the posts and there is no stud wall cavity for conduit and other wiring, we realized during planning that many holes would have to be drilled in the posts to carry electrical conduit laterally around the building for power and communications. These holes could not be gnawed out of the back edge of the posts — they would need to be deeper into the meat of the wood. Every conduit's transit of a post would have to first sweep out and then sweep back to the wall surface. This would add work and expense; plus, all those holes weaken and deface the wood.

We proposed instead that the posts have two-inch blocking applied to the back, leaving three designated spaces at typical code-required heights for electrical installations to pass through. Thus, the posts seem to float off the wall, allowing them to appear fully three-dimensional.

In woodworking and construction, a small space separating two materials is often called a "reveal." Sometimes it's a groove, or what the British sometimes call a "quirk." In this case, the reveal itself does indeed reveal the structure and keep the components separate... but connected, unblemished, and whole.

These simple and elegant measures, born of exposed connections and careful planning, literally reveal the structure and meaning of the building, the way knuckles and shoulders tell us about human bodies.

The Eighteen-Inch Drop

WE SAT IN THE PRESIDENT'S OFFICE AT
HAMPSHIRE COLLEGE AS THE R.W. KERN CENTER
NEARED COMPLETION. THE R.W. KERN CENTER TEAM
had been asked to participate with Hampshire College in a half-day conversation
about sustainability with a major corporation. It was an opportunity for influence,
not fundraising. Perhaps we could be useful as Bruner/Cott Architects helped
the corporation plan a major shift in its focus and its headquarters' location.

Something in the Living Building Challenge process itself calls forth a deeper and different awareness, one that is organized organically and internally. As people who manage ideas, documents, work, concepts, and risks, the team is presumed to have a mental roll-aboard containing all such news, information, and documentation. But knowledge does not necessarily advance along that path. Something from another brain hemisphere was in motion, written in a different hand.

Jason Forney from Bruner/Cott mentioned that the most important foundation for the R.W. Kern Center project process was an early commitment to clear project goals. These had been drafted, discussed, and edited in great detail. The College's entire building committee had been involved, including design team members, staff, faculty, and students. The rest of us on the team nodded.

Our visitors, their curiosity piqued, asked us what the project goals were. We looked at Jason, he looked at his project partner, Jason Jewhurst, and they warbled a bit about general themes. None of us had brought our script, and for the life of us we could not remember the specific language. After a moment of embarrassment, Jason assured our guests that he would forward the text of the goals, and that we had lived by them daily. They had lodged themselves so deeply in us that we could not recite the words on command.

Something in the Living Building Challenge process itself calls forth a deeper and different awareness, one that is organized organically and internally. As people who manage ideas, documents, work, concepts, and risks, the team is presumed to have a mental roll-aboard containing all such news, information, and documentation. But knowledge does not necessarily advance along that path. Something from another brain hemisphere was in motion, written in a different hand.

A few weeks after participating in the sustainability conversation, I was sharing this story with my old friend Paul Foster Moore, a skilled psychotherapist and clinician. He listened and then said, "Ah, the eighteen-inch drop." He went on to describe a condition and circumstance he had seen often enough in his professional practice that he had given it a name. The eighteen-inch drop, he explained, is this: We assemble and develop an idea, and as we come to know it longer and more deeply, it gradually embeds itself in the thoracic area of the lungs and heart.

These deep air- and blood-filled regions of the body — located approximately eighteen inches below our brains — do not know how to speak well on their own. So many important thoughts and ideas reside there, as well as passions, sorrows, and instincts. But much of our power to communicate about them gets lost en route to the surface. It is a region of genius, where the most skilled artisans, tradespeople, dancers, musicians, and writers keep their most valuable knowledge. It houses the wisdom that makers know "like the backs of our hands."

Understanding the eighteen-inch drop eased my mind about why we were all at a loss for words in that meeting at the College. The startled moment of lost recall was renamed, acknowledging its deep, robust, core placement in each of us.

When the architects returned to their office, they opened the document containing the text of the R.W. Kern Center goals:

1. The R.W. Kern Center will ensure that prospective students discover the Hampshire education more directly. Prospective students will experience a stronger sense of arrival at the center of the campus to begin their visit. The building will provide a framework for showcasing current student projects, along with faculty and alumni work (books, films, music, art), inspiring prospects to follow in their footsteps.

2. Meeting a variety of space needs, the R.W. Kern Center will be a place that encourages community, collaboration, and conversation.

3. The building will enhance the Admissions process and relieve limitations imposed by current buildings. It will provide adequate and continuous space for Admissions staff, improving information flow and more opportunities to discuss prospective students to gather. It will be a comfortable and engaging place for families to gather while exploring the Hampshire community.

4. The project will push the boundaries of environmental design by achieving "Living status" under the Living Building Challenge. The Challenge is the most ambitious green building standard we know. Hampshire adopts the Challenge's rigorous goals with respect to human well-being, net zero energy, net zero water, leading edge materials thinking, and minimizing environmental impacts. The Challenge underscores Hampshire's core commitment to the environment.

5. The R.W. Kern Center should convey Hampshire College's values, and help tell the story of a unique, progressive, and experimenting intellectual community. The architecture should provide space for new ways of learning, and include space to interactively showcase the work of others, present and past.

6. The architecture of the building should belong in its context, one of New England farmhouses and "brutalist" modern architecture, mountain views, and valley vistas. The building should be organized to frame its natural setting. The Hampshire community has used the following words and phrases to describe the look and feel of the building: striking and new, impressive but not pretentious, vibrant, and connected to the outdoors.

7. The design should be accessible, flexible, and adaptable.

8. The landscape should invite people to be around the R.W. Kern Center, not just inside it. Hampshire students and faculty enjoy being outside. Spaces in the landscape around the building are equally important for community building and letting prospective students know that the outdoors are an important part of the Hampshire experience.

9. Design and decision making should be a collaborative process that yields good results while allowing input, investigation, and inquiry. The design and construction processes should be a learning opportunity for the College administration, staff, faculty, and students.

Two sets of air-source heat pumps take care of all the climate control, and hum along pretty much like refrigerators.

I Do Radio

"DON'T YOU HAVE ANYTHING HERE THAT MAKES NOISE? IT'S SO QUIET!" I WAS TAKING KAREN BROWN, A REPORTER from New England Public Radio, on a walking tour around the R.W. Kern Center and we were strolling the perimeter of the building. I pointed to the Mitsubishi heat pump condensers, whose soft purrs complemented the rustle of a few nearby leaves. "Why do we need noise?" I asked.

She looked at me with a wry smile, holding up her big puppet-head-sized puffy microphone. "I do radio, Jonathan!" she said.

Beginning our interior tour, we paused in the atrium, where a couple of big-blade ceiling fans turned lazily overhead. The Kern Kafé coffee bar was closed for the afternoon, but a few tables in the atrium were occupied with people softly chatting, quietly reading, or gently tapping on laptop keys.

"Let's go to the basement," I suggested, leading the way to the dead-quiet Kone electric elevator that would take us to the lowest level. I began telling Karen that electric elevators use one-third the power of hydraulic units, and there is no need for the large mechanical rooms with noisy pumps. Plus, the Living Building Challenge does not allow the use of hydraulic fluid because it contains phthalates. All this is good news from an environmental standpoint, but bad news for a radio reporter searching for noise in a noiseless elevator.

The elevator doors closed behind us silently after we stepped into the basement. I said, "Welcome to the deafening silence of our stinky, greasy basement!" Of course, there was no smell, no grease, and no sound here except one greywater pump, quieter than a washing machine behind a closed door.

Karen looked around, taking in the big black Clivis Multrum composting toilet bins. Down a hallway, she saw

NEAR RIGHT:
No sounds of flush toilets here.

FAR RIGHT:
Elevator machine rooms without hydraulic pumps. The R.W. Kern Center elevators are electric, and counter balanced. They are whisper quiet and use 80% less power.

solar inverters lining the far wall, silently converting the direct-current solar electricity into alternating current for building use. Then she spotted four men in tee shirts and jeans across the room. They were contractors, all on laptops, checking specifications and detailed technical operating instructions and requirements for different equipment. They looked at their screens and conversed quietly.

She went over to one of the workers and introduced herself, digging deeper for some kind of clamor. It went something like this:

"Hi, I'm Karen Brown from NEPR. What's your name and what are you working on?"

"I'm Patrick O'Conner, the mechanical foreman for M. J. Moran."

"What did you do here on the R.W. Kern Center project?"

"I laid out and coordinated all of the mechanical systems, ductwork, piping, refrigeration, and water."

"Wow. What was the hardest thing about working on this project?"

"Just getting the stuff we needed. It was really hard to keep the work flow going, waiting for materials and parts."

(pause)

"Well, would you do it again?"

"Oh, yeah, definitely, in a heartbeat."

"But, if it was so hard, why would you want to do it again?"

(no pause)

"Because it was so interesting!"

Patrick was brought to the Kern project by his boss, Jim Moran, founder of M. J. Moran. As part of his own introduction to the Living Building Challenge, Jim had attended our pre-construction planning mini-conference months earlier to learn about our goals for this revolutionary building. Jim had spent his early work years leaning over a Bunsen burner melting lead for old-fashioned lead-and-oakum iron waste pipe joints. Like virtually everyone who started out in the trades (myself included), Jim was exposed to chemical hazards almost every day. All of us have since seen colleagues and coworkers succumb to the effects of industrial poisons.

Leaving the conference after a full day gaining a first grasp of what we were working to accomplish with the Living Building Challenge, Jim turned to me and asked, "Jonathan, why didn't we do this twenty years ago?"

I wish Karen Brown could have also captured Jim's optimism on her microphone the way she later captured Patrick's. Together, their voices and those of the hundreds of makers who have come to understand the importance and urgency of working to reduce toxins in construction materials make quite a chorus.

Sparkle

"JONATHAN, I JUST LOVE HOW IT SPARKLES!" I LOOKED UP, NOTICING FOR THE FIRST TIME HOW THE POLISHED aluminum curved fan blades captured, spread, and released the light. "Well, Lee," I said with a grin. "It was the best we could do because we couldn't use the black ones that were specified because of questions about the finish chemistry."

Slowly rotating Big Ass Fans gently destratify the air in the R.W. Kern Center atrium, their blades shining in the sunlight.

What I have noticed about Lee is what she notices about life: the small details and the big picture. The R.W. Kern Center brings her great joy not only in its grand and dignified remembrance of her husband, but in the many details of design and workmanship that reflect talent and care.

Lee Kern had just walked deliberately but briskly up the stairs of the R.W. Kern Center, the Living Building that bears her late husband's name. She stopped and took in the view of the place from the second-floor gallery, her blue eyes bright and full of curiosity and delight. As she looked out over the opening toward the Kern Kafé and atrium below, one of the two Big Ass Fans — yes, that's a brand name — turning slowly in the mottled sunshine caught her eye.

The metal parts of the R.W. Kern Center, including rails, window parts, curtain walls, and concrete aggregate, are all black. It made sense that the fans would be finished in satin black. But compliance information on the black paint was just not available, so we had to settle for the more expensive polished aluminum. Throughout the Living Building Challenge process, coatings, finishes, and colors require careful examination due to chemical content of pigments, solvents, and dryers. It turns out that many decorative coatings are comprised of toxic elements and, as such, have no place in a Living Building, or anywhere else for that matter.

Instead of being a graceful but unobtrusive mechanical device, the aluminum finish transformed the fans into pieces of structural whimsy, light refraction, and sculpture. It's what we got as an "upgrade" because of what we could NOT have. The lessons run deep in Lee Kern's exuberant embrace of what she saw.

As we headed back downstairs via the elevator, I launched into a recitation of my thin knowledge of the wonders of the Kone

balanced electric elevator. It needs no oil reservoir and uses less than one-third the electricity of the conventional hydraulic type equipment. Before I had gotten very far into the second sentence of my commentary, she said, "Oh, yes. That's all we use in our buildings in New York," and then continued on with some off-hand and extensive technical details. So much to learn at each visit and conversation with this extraordinary woman.

When noted New York architect Bruce Fowle toured the building, he commented that the balanced electric elevator is the most efficient form of transportation made by humans. All that is required is the energy to counteract the weight of the payload, and only on the up-trip. Not quite perpetual motion, but close.

Months after Lee had admired the beautiful fans, when the water system for the R.W. Kern Center was up for a trial run of site-produced drinking water — provisionally approved by both the Massachusetts Department of Environmental Protection (DEP) and the Federal Environmental Protection Agency (EPA) — Lee Kern and Bill Kern came up for a visit.

We learned that day what water tastes like when nothing is added or taken away. It tastes like, well, nothing at all. It is just a smooth, fluid oral experience, free of chlorine, stabilizers, or any added minerals. It comes to us just the way it falls from the sky, with only a little side trip through paper filters and an ozonator!

Lee loved it. We sat below one of the fans and raised a compostable paper cup to toast another achievement: pure water, still but sparkling, marking the integration of a design and construction experiment into daily life. The water in our hands had traveled from ocean to cloud, to stream, to roof, then to reservoir, and to pipe — moving, gurgling, in drips and torrents along the way. Overhead, the fan moved the air silently. We could feel how the air and the water were balanced in that great atrium space.

What I have noticed about Lee is what she notices about life: the small details and the big picture. The R.W. Kern Center brings her great joy not only in its grand and dignified remembrance of her husband, but in the many details of design and workmanship that reflect talent and care. And the liveliness there is all about Lee. Like her, the place just sparkles.

Leona Kern is completely at home in the R.W. Kern Center, which bears both her late husband's name and her own lasting signature warmth and intelligence.

EPILOGUE:

Why on Earth

Why on earth would we choose to set out on a journey as complex, mystifying, and time-consuming as the Living Building Challenge? People ask me that question often. Isn't greener really green enough?

My answers live, at least in part, in the pages of this book. Why would we not strive to understand and meet the Challenge? It is a welcome and open invitation to explore, to be uncertain, vulnerable, and resourceful. The process is inhabited by inspired, talented, experienced, and supportive people with enviable design and human values, engaged in changing the way everything in the world is made based on understanding how the world is actually made. Why shuffle along when we can stride? Why just watch when we can touch and embrace and make a measurable difference?

My own maker's journey began early in life and continues every day. The opportunities to connect with these buildings and their people has reinforced my commitment to the craft of making. The experience of learning and being coached in the writing of this book is deep and unforgettable, for which I am very grateful.

Particularly because of how close I came to missing out on it all.

In the week following my first trip with the R.W. Kern Center team to Seattle in late 2013, testing confirmed an advanced aortic valve diagnosis that required nearly immediate open-heart surgery. I was healthy and athletic, but new sobering risks were at hand. I was instructed to move slowly and walk for transportation purposes only until surgery could be arranged a few weeks hence.

When the procedure was complete, I talked with my surgeon, Dr. Umer Darr at Yale New Haven Hospital, thanking him for his amazing work, accomplishing a cutting and sewing job on something the size of a chopstick's tip. He said, "No, Jonathan, we've done the easy part. Now it is your time. Your body has withstood about as much as it can, and over the next weeks you may become discouraged. All the enzymes in your body will be scavenging for protein and re-building materials to help you heal. You will feel weaker for some weeks until, one day, you will feel a bit better."

I have pondered this natural healing and regenerative design that my body accomplished over those next months, marveling at what human nature can do with no power tools or internet! It's just our own biochemistry at work. I attended R.W. Kern Center building committee meetings holding my red compression cushion to my chest as a man in the process of

being reborn. I literally experienced being rebuilt in a new restorative way, just as I was beginning to learn how the Living Building Challenge asks us to seek a regenerative relationship with the earth from which we draw life and strength. As my bones slowly grew back where they had been cut, I realized the oyster that processes algae in cold water in order to make a porcelain shell is more my kin that I had ever imagined.

My view of what is possible in the human body and in human endeavor were changed forever during the years producing these two Living Buildings. No longer able to accept good-enough solutions, I keep coming back to the core work of makers everywhere: to make everything better. I am more torn and incensed by the senseless mess humans continue to make of our world, while being ever more committed to leaning into the work that will help us all change course.

We have changed course. We can feel the tug on the tiller. We have demonstrated that net zero water, waste, and energy are possible and cost effective in cold climates. These buildings pay operating dividends every month of the year, year after year. Together, we have shown that local and regional materials add beauty and value while shrinking costs and carbon footprints. We have shown that eliminating finishes not only

saves money but inspires occupants, builders, designers, and visitors alike to engage with the character of the place itself.

The buildings live in their places just as the places inhabit their buildings, in a conversation that will continue for generations. We have shown how buildings create movement, emotional content, contentment, and inspiration. We have created footholds, and are roped in. The climb is long but the terrain beautiful, the company excellent, and the incline manageable.

Every day, each of us can make choices to heal the earth, refine our work, and refresh our vision to focus on "What does good look like?"

Just like that. Why on earth? Because the work of makers is unmatched in beauty and utility, and carries the spirit and markings of the best that humans can do.

The Living Building Challenge: An Overview

The Living Building Challenge was developed as a game-changing green building certification program and sustainable design framework. It visualizes the ideal for the built environment as a key contributor to the rejuvenation and health of the world's natural systems and inhabitants. These aspirations carry hope and urgency for the program's participants and for the Planet.

It uses the metaphor of a gerbera daisy because the ideal built environment should function as cleanly and efficiently as a flower. Living Buildings give more than they take, creating a positive impact on the human and natural systems that interact with them.

The Living Building Challenge offers standards and guidance for new construction, renovation, and landscapes. The focus reaches beyond doing less harm, and asks, "What does good look like?"

THERE ARE TWO CORE RULES FOR THE LIVING BUILDING CHALLENGE:

1. All Imperatives assigned to a Typology, or general classification of project types, are mandatory because the Challenge asks everyone to reach and seek total, integrated solutions.

2. Certification requires actual documented, rather than anticipated, performance demonstrated over twelve consecutive months. This ensures proper commissioning, and keeps teams focused on how buildings really work. The process is accountable and revealing, thriving on goals rather than gates.

The Living Building Challenge is organized into seven performance areas called Petals. Each Petal is further sub-divided into Imperatives, which address specific issues through detailed requirements. All of the Petals reach beyond individual buildings, scrutinizing sources, processes, and chemicals used in manufacturing. This deeper focus on workforce and occupant well-being is unique to the Challenge and resonates with trades and craftspeople.

Both Living Buildings that stand on the Hampshire College campus were designed, constructed, and audited under Version 2.1 of the Challenge, which contained the following Petals and Imperatives:

Living Building Challenge Petals, interpreted at the Hitchcock Center

PETAL	IMPERATIVES
SITE	Limits to Growth
	Urban Agriculture
	Habitat Exchange (When we develop, we must set aside more than we consume, to ensure all creatures can thrive.)
	Car Free Living
WATER	**Net Zero Water** (The site must harvest and produce its own drinking and process water.)
	Ecological Water Flow (Requires restoration of ground water and reduction in stormwater.)
ENERGY	**Net Zero Energy** (The building must generate at least as much energy as it uses over the course of a year.)
HEALTH	Civilized Environment
	Healthy Air
	Biophilia (Buildings and systems reflect and celebrate our affinity for the natural world.)
MATERIALS	**Red List** (Eliminating the use of many of the most egregious toxins from our products and workplaces.)
	Embodied Carbon Footprint (Calculates the carbon released as a result of the materials and construction processes.)
	Responsible Industry
	Appropriate Sourcing (Based on environmental, human resource, and proximity standards.)
	Conservation + Reuse
EQUITY	Human Scale + Humane Places
	Democracy + Social Justice
	Rights to Nature (Access to natural places and environments is a requirement for human health.)
BEAUTY	Beauty + Spirit
	Inspiration + Education

The Makers

These are the people who appear in the pages of this book, part of the vast group who contributed their skills and energy.

Name	Project Role	Affiliation	R.W.K.C.	H.C.E.
Johanna Andersen-Pratt	Co-owner of stone quarry and head of the stone fabrication facility.	Ashfield Stone Company	x	
Phil Andrikidis	Owner and crew chief of the roofing company for both buildings.	Florence Roofing	x	x
Larry Archey	Director of Facilities at the College, and in charge of the overall development and maintenance of the campus. Much loved and highly respected member of the campus and larger communities.	Hampshire College	x	x
John Averill	Foreman; in charge of all on-site methods, staffing, safety, and procurement.	Wright Builders, Inc.	x	
Sam Batchelor	Co-leader of design team; planned the project approach and concept design, systems, and built the design team.	designLAB architects		x
Vladimir Bondar	Masonry contractor who also laid up stone and facilitated the stone work.	Vladimir Bondar Masonry	x	
CJ Brehio	Foreman; directed all aspects of timber and decking erection.	Bensonwood	x	
Karen Brown	Reporter who came to the nearly-finished building and filed a great story.	New England Public Radio	x	
Lisa Carey Moore	Sustainability manager; part of the materials team.	Integrated Eco Strategy	x	x
Chris Chamberland	Civil engineer who designed the water systems.	The Berkshire Design Group, Inc.	x	x
Christina Cianfrani	Assistant Professor of Hydrology; part of teaching team that designed curriculum and research around the R.W. Kern Center.	Hampshire College	x	
Patrick Coffey	Owner of painting company that did the finishes on both buildings.	Coffey & Heady Painting	x	x
Bruce Coldham	Amherst architect who first introduced us at Wright Builders to the Challenge and advised Bruner/Cott.	Coldham & Hartman Architects	x	
Jamie Crocker	Owner; oversaw electrical materials and installation on both projects, embracing the Challenge.	Crocker Communications Inc.	x	x
Alejandro Cuellar	Writing instructor and Faculty Associate.	Hampshire College	x	

Name	Project Role	Affiliation	R.W.K.C.	H.C.E.
Daniel de Wit	Owner and artist; designed and executed the etched flooring design at the Hitchcock Center.	EnnisArt		x
Megan Dobro	Assistant Professor of Biology; part of teaching team that designed curriculum and research around the R.W. Kern Center.	Hampshire College	x	
Sara Draper	Architects' liaison for all materials vetting and tracking; liaison for all Living Building documentation.	Bruner/Cott Architects	x	
Paul Foster Moore	Inventor of the "Eighteen-Inch Drop" concept and long-time friend of the author.		x	
Jason Forney	Senior architect involved in planning, goal articulation, and concept designing.	Bruner/Cott Architects	x	
Bruce Fowle	Architect and friend of the Kern family who visited the R.W. Kern Center with keen interest.	The Fowle Collaborative		
Richie Frend	Project assistant; worked on materials vetting.	Wright Builders, Inc.	x	
Michael Frost	Owner; directed and performed the grinding, polishing, and sealing of concrete floors at the R.W. Kern Center.	Vermont Eco-Floors	x	
Linda Gaudreau	Operations Manager; oversaw all materials procurement and staffing needs, and supplies procurement, including cider donuts and almonds.	Wright Builders, Inc.	x	x
Nil Gaudreau	Linda Gaudreau's dad, a chemical factory worker			
Kelly Ard Haigh	Co-leader of design team; planned the project and executed the bulk of the design documents, including materials research and systems; built the design team.	designLAB architects		x
Tom Harris	Owner and technical genius.	Architectural Timber & Millwork, Inc.	x	
Sarah Hews	Assistant Professor of Mathematics; part of teaching team that designed curriculum and research around the R.W. Kern Center.	Hampshire College	x	
Todd Holland	Mechanical engineer who oversaw many energy upgrades en route to carbon neutral on the Hampshire campus.	Hampshire College	x	
Jason Jewhurst	Architect who worked as primary project manager; oversaw construction detailing, permitting and compliance processes, coordination with design consultants, and coordination with the construction team for the architect.	Bruner/Cott Architects	x	
Julie Johnson	Executive Director; spearheaded the decision to strive for a Living Building as an environmental benchmark and unique teaching tool.	Hitchcock Center for the Environment		x

Name	Project Role	Affiliation	R.W.K.C.	H.C.E.
Colleen Kelly	Education Director for all programs; part of project planning team.	Hitchcock Center for the Environment		x
Bill Kern	Sponsor, advisor, advocate, champion.		x	
Leona Kern	Sponsor, advocate, champion.		x	
Ralph Kern	R.W. Kern Center namesake.		x	
Matt Kirchman	Principal and designer of educational tools and displays.	ObjectIDEA		x
Rick Klein	Principal and lead campus design planner; oversaw the water systems design.	The Berkshire Design Group, Inc.	x	
Jay Klemyk	Machine operator and layout foreman for sitework on both projects.	Karl's Sitework	x	x
Katie Koerten	Children, Youth and Family Programs Coordinator; part of project planning team.	Hitchcock Center for the Environment		x
Bob Kuda	Sheet metal and ductwork technician.	Northeastern Sheetmetal Co. Inc.	x	
Jonathan Lash	Hampshire's President, who challenged the College to think big and boldly through advancing an environmentally sustainable campus concept, including inviting the Hitchcock Center to the campus.	Hampshire College	x	x
Ann Ledwell	Assistant Project Manager who worked on materials vetting, organized procurement and supplies, mostly for the Hitchcock Center.	Wright Builders, Inc.	x	x
Mark Ledwell	Vice President and co-owner of Wright Builders, and primary project manager for the Hitchcock Center construction, including procurement, staffing, and contract administration. Provided overall team leadership across both projects.	Wright Builders, Inc.	x	x
Chuck Longsworth	Co-founder, former president, and lifelong advocate of Hampshire College.	Hampshire College		
Tom Lucia	Project Manager; in charge of design interpretation, procurement, materials, subcontracts, scheduling, and project leadership.	Wright Builders, Inc.	x	
Cath McKusker	Senior member, materials team.	Integrated Eco Strategy	x	x
Andrew Meyer	Owner and founder of innovative green finishes company in Vermont that utilizes waste cheese whey for their products.	Vermont Natural Coatings, Inc.	x	x
Joe Miles	Owner, who went the extra mile to support lumber supplies for both projects.	r.k. MILES Building Materials Supplier	x	x

Name	Project Role	Affiliation	R.W.K.C.	H.C.E.
Guilford Mooring	Public Works chief in Amherst who embraced the Challenge and gave us early direct guidance on how to ensure public water quality safety in the buildings.	Town of Amherst	X	X
Jim Moran	Mechanical contractor who embraced the Challenge and helped set the tone for the project.	M. J. Moran, Inc.	X	
Rebecca Neimark	Development Director; facilitated the raising of funds; part of project planning team.	Hitchcock Center for the Environment		X
Erik Anders Nelson	Structural engineer who prompted collaboration and innovation in the building structure.	Structures Workshop, Inc.		X
Petro ("Peter") Nepeyvoda	Mason who laid up much of the R.W. Kern Center exterior stone work.	Vladimir Bondar Masonry	X	
Christopher Nielsen	Architect who was primary designer and draftsman, then primary on-site design representative.	Bruner/Cott Architects	X	
Patrick O'Conner	Mechanical foreman who oversaw all the duct, machinery, piping, and plumbing layouts, as well as executing plumbers' work.	M. J. Moran, Inc.	X	
Vassily Ohremenko	Mason who worked on the R.W. Kern Center.	Vladimir Bondar Masonry	X	
Patrick O'Roark	Environmental educator for children and adults.	Hitchcock Center for the Environment		X
Brandon Osman	Stone artisan.	Ashfield Stone Company	X	
Rob Pytko	Expert journeyman plumber.	Dobert Heating and Air Conditioning		X
Chris Riddle	Retired co-founder of Kuhn Riddle Architects; worked as owner's representative on the Hitchcock Center construction.			X
Steven Roof	Professor of Earth Sciences; part of teaching team that designed curriculum and research around the R.W. Kern Center.	Hampshire College	X	
Marc Rosenbaum	Energy systems modeling, design, planning, and testing for the R.W. Kern Center, who also consulted on the Hitchcock Center.	South Mountain Company, Inc.	X	X
Alexander Schreyer	Senior lecturer; consulted on wood technologies, methods, and wood performance during construction.	University of Massachusetts, Amherst	X	
Jessica Schultz	Communications and Living Building Coordinator; part of project planning team.	Hitchcock Center for the Environment		X
Tom Schulz	Owner and artist; designed and executed the etched flooring design.	EnnisArt		X

Name	Project Role	Affiliation	R.W.K.C.	H.C.E.
Helen Ann Sephton	School Programs Coordinator; part of project planning team.	Hitchcock Center for the Environment		x
Jesse Sheldon	Foreman in charge of fitting and installing the curtain wall and windows.	R&R Windows Contractors Inc.	x	
Marcus Simon	Development Coordinator; supported the fundraising program needs; part of project planning team.	Hitchcock Center for the Environment		x
Jim Small	Foreman in charge of all on-site methods, staffing, safety, and procurement.	Wright Builders, Inc.	x	
Andrew Solem	Assistant Project Manager; in charge of materials vetting, supplies, and relationships with manufacturers.	Wright Builders, Inc.	x	x
Mark Spiro	Chief Financial Officer during the planning of the projects.	Hampshire College	x	x
Charlie Stevenson	Principal; guided the whole materials process.	Integrated Eco Strategy	x	x
Ashley Sullivan	Geotechnical engineer.	O'Reilly, Talbot and Okun Engineering Associates		x
Mike Talbot	Principal and geotechnical engineer.	O'Reilly, Talbot and Okun Engineering Associates		x
Brian Tetreault	Truss designer; developed the working plans for fabrication of the complex wood roof structural systems.	Universal Forest Products Inc.	x	x
Jason Tor	Associate Professor of Biology; part of teaching team that designed curriculum and research around the R.W. Kern Center.	Hampshire College	x	
Kerry Uhler	Managed the fabrication and installation of timberwork.	Bensonwood	x	
Carl Weber	Primary owner's representative and project manager, managing scope of design and construction, cost, and systems.	Hampshire College	x	
Jonathan Wright	Principal; responsible for overall constructability strategies, systems review, planning, and budgeting at both projects, and worked as project executive on the R.W. Kern Center.	Wright Builders, Inc.	x	x
Barnaby Young	Electrical foreman; in charge of planning, layout, and workmanship.	Crocker Communications Inc.	x	x

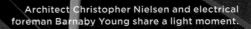
Architect Christopher Nielsen and electrical foreman Barnaby Young share a light moment.

It's how we're wired.

All Hands Honor Roll: R.W. Kern Center

A compilation of all those who touched the project in some way, from fundraising, to gifts, to labor, to design, with apologies if your name was overlooked.

April Abner
Alan Ackerman
Jon Adams
Rachelle Ain
Brian Aja
Chris Allard
Marc S. Allen
Justin Allenbee
Dina Amouzigh
Diane Amsterdam
Jim Anderson
Laurie Anderson
Johanna Anderson-Pratt
Phil Andrikidis
Gabriel Arboleda
Joseph Arce
Lawrence M. Archey
Carolyn Anne Arnold
Matthew Arnold
Seth Ashworth
Henry Waldorf Astor
Leslie Astor
John Averall
K.T. Baldassaro
Frank Baldino
Clay Ballantine
Joanna S. Ballantine
Jon Bander
Denise Banister
Manish Bapna
Eric Barnes
Brian Barrett
Jeff Bean
Steve Beckwith
Fraser Bennet Beede
Rachid Belhocine

Tedd Benson
Robert Berard
Carol Amy Bergman
Jean Bergman
Richard Bernard, Jr.
Steve Best
Mame Bisaccio
Kevin Bittenbender
Nate Black
Scott Blanger
Paul Boa
Vladimir Bondar
Brad Bordewieck
Marion Borko
Judy Naomi Bornstein
Marco Boscardin
Mario Boucher
Tammy Boutwell
Iver Bowen
Robin Braman
CJ Brehio
Myrna Margulies Breitbart
William Breitbart
Benjamin Brennan
Christine Brestrup
Joe Brosseau
Kristin Brosseau
Jillian T. Brown
Joanna Lillian
Shawn Brown
Terrence Brown
Scott Bryant
Taylor Buchalter
Jonathan Buell
Michael Buell
John Buhl

Skip Burck
Sandra J. Burgess
Jonathan Burnett
Cheryl Atwood Butler
Roger Buzzell
Barton Byg
Almando Caez
Melissa Caldwell
Nolan Campbell
Chris Carbone
Kyle Cardaropoli
Cheryl Carey
Lisa Carey Moore
Shelley Johnson Carey
Holly Carlson
Harold J. Carroll
Paul Casavant
Edward Cavanaugh
Ryan Chaffee
Chris Chamberland
Mike Chambers
Lisa Chang
Joe Charter
David Chase
Asher Chicoine
Kevin Childs
Myron Chudzik
Stephine Ciccarello
Adam Clark
Andy Clogston
David Cody
Joe Coffey
Pat Coffey
Helen Scheuer Cohen
Madeleine Atkins Cohen
Bruce Coldham
Jeff Coleman
Jack Cominoli
George Cone
Elizabeth Conlisk
Roger Cooney
Heather Corbett
Rick Corriveau

Richard Costa
Walter Costa
Jamie Crocker
Kearsten Crocker
John Crosby, Sr.
F. Bennett Cushman
Hal Cutler
Cory Dale
Susan Marie Darlington
Mark Darnold
Thomas K. Davies
Troy A.W. Davis
Grant Dawson
Jason Daysh
Steven Daysh
Andree L. De Lisser
Michael Deane
Edward Churchwell Dees
Ronald Demers
Rheannon DeMond
Alex Desaulneirs
Thomas Devine
Michael Dezinno
Jampa Dhundup
David Dinerman
Lucy Dion
Juan Dominguez
Jake Donahue
McKay Donald
Lobsang Dorjee
Rhonda Dossett
Stanton Evans Dossett
Sara Draper
L. Pasha Dritt Thorton
Elizabeth Dromey
Smauel Duffy
Marjorie R. Dunehew
Michelle Dykstra
Linda Ann Earle
Alex Echevarria
Tom Edgerton
Leanna Beth Einbinder
Terry Eldred

Kenneth Engerman
Maryelizabeth Fahey
Valerie Faille
Charles Fendt
Jason Ferland
Yaniris Fernandez
Bram George Fierstein
Jocelyn Fillion
Don Finefrock
Shana Marion Fisher
Lanette D. Fisher-Hertz
Russell Fishkind
David Fisk
Nathan Fletcher
Richard Florek
Susan Flynn
Jason Forney
Jason Fortier
Tom Foster
Scott Frazier
Renee Ellen Freedman
Richard French
Richard Frend
Sascha Darius Freudenheim
Marlene Gerber Fried
Walter Fritz
Colin Frost
Karen Frost
Michael Frost
Jose Andres Fuentes
Austin Fuller
Bill Fuller
Cody Fuller
Roger Fuller
Tim Fuller
Justin G.
Scott G.
Michael Gagne
Suzanna Gal Gombos
Gail Gatton
Linda Gaudreau
Keri Gauvin
Megan Smith Gendreau

Caryl Giard
Larry Giard
David J. Gibson
Dustin Gilbert
Nancy Gilbert
Kim Gladding
Jonathan Glick
Adam Golash
Joseph Gomez
Lisa Goodwin Robbins
Zach Goodwin-Boyd
Benjamin Gormely
Lori J. Gould
Nancy Graham
Parvati Maggie Grais
Dave Granger
Linda J. Green
Corwin E. Greenberg
Karne Greene
Carolyn Greenspan
J. Christopher Groobey
Brandon Grover
Adam Gunn
Gueorgui Hadjiysky
Seth Hagar
Barbara Cashman Hahn
Steven Jonathan Hahn
Matthew Halstead
Tom Hancock
Mark Hanks
Sarah A. Hart-Agudelo
Dorothy H. and Frederick J.
    Haug Family Foundation
Thomas Hayden
Peter Hechenbleikner
Jay Heilman
Lily Frances Henderson
Scott Henderson
Dave Hennessey
Philip Henry
Luis Antonio Hernandez
Paul Hewes
Gaye Hill

Rick Hinton
Louise E. Hodges
Joe Hodnicki
Josh Hoffman
Tom Holden
S. Rebecca Holland
Dylan Stuart Holmes
Mia Homan
Bethanie A. Hooker
Thomas Hotaling
Emily Nora Hubley
Sam Hughes
James Hunkler
Beau Hurlburt
Roger Hutchins
George Monks Hutchinson
Jenna Rae Kohles Hutchinson
Evan Iannoli
Mariye Inouye
Justin Jackson
Sarah Jackson
David Jalbert
Mary Beth James
Andrew Michael Janiak
Myrt Jaquay-Wilson
Shane Jernigan
Jason Jewhurst
Alec Jillson
Candace Johnson
Eric Johnson
Jonathan Jordan
Stephan Friederich Jost
Alex Kaleyin
Mark Kalin
Nancy Karella
Elizabeth Keary
Brendan Keenan
Christian Kehl
Andrea Kelleher
Bob Kelley
Jeremy Kellogg
Mickey Kellogg
Dana Kelly

Sue Kennedy
Franklin Kern
Leona Klein Kern
William Daniel Kern
Greg Kilbride
Sean Kim
Scott Kirkendall
Michael T. Klare
Whitney Wilder Klare
Rick Klein
Jay Klemyk
Christopher H. Knauf
Tomas Kocis
Dan Kokonowski
Timothy M. Koller
Alan Konieczny
Steven Konieczny
Justin Kopacz
Robert Korzec
Carl Koslowski
Matthew Robert Krefting
Alex David Kreit
Chris Krezmian
Patricia Krieg
Zachary Kurimay
Chris L.
Becky Lacaprucia
Jeff Lacaprucia
Lisa Laflamme
Mike Lagasse
Marianne Lampke
AJ Lapinski
Clayton Lapointe
Brian Laprade
Daniel Larison
Adam Laroche
Russ Laroche
Jonathan Lash
Brian Latham
Jennifer Garratt Lawton
Jeffrey Leclair
Ryan Leduc
Ann Ledwell

Luke Ledwell
Mark Ledwell
Elane Dorothy Lee
Edward Lenois
Thomas Lentilhon
Jay Lepple
Sura Levine
Dan Lewis
Greg Lewis
Tyler Lewis
Will Lewis
Brad Liljequist
Steven Lily
Mai Line Villemin
Lisa Linnehan
Josiah Shafran Litant
Brian Llewelyn
Daniel Longe
Larry Longe, Jr.
Michael Longo
Gregg Joseph Loubier
Leslie Ann Loubier
Tom Lucia
John Luszcz
Ed M.
Derek Mallery
Steven Mallery, II
Nathaniel Malloy
Steven Manard
John Manganaro
Rick Manser
Sierra Marcks
Dennis Marcom
Aaron Marcus
Julie Marcus
Nikos Marmaras
Isaac Levin Marshall
Bob Martel
Julie A. Martel
Christopher Martin
David H. Matheson
Richmond Mayo-Smith
David Mazor

Stanley Mazor
Helen McCabe
Josh McCarthy
Robert McCarthy
Jeffrey McComb
Kath McCusker
Shari McDaid
John McElroy
Lucy-Ann McFadden
Doug McGill
Michael W. McKenna
Jason McNair
Michael Meadows
Theresa Meckel
Alejandra Mendez-Rivera
Doug Mercier
Deborah Marie Merrill-Sands
Kathleen M. Methot
Robert L. Methot
Faisal Irfan Mian
Peter Miccoli
Robert Mikalunas
Jean D. Miller
Lynn Miller
Melissa Erin Mills-Dick
Glen Mimerstorf
John Mitchell
Paul Russel Model
Susan Monahan
Matthew Montague
James Mooney
Guilford Mooring
Luis Morales
Jim Moran
Daniel Moriarty
Rob Morra
Henry Moss
Don Mulhern
Patrick Murphy
John Musante
Peter N.
Andrew Nadolski
Nicholas Nash

Laura Calamos Nasir
Tariq Nasir
Patrick Neal
Valerie Nelson
W. Tim Nelson
Michael Nelson
John Niedbala
Christopher Nielsen
Paige Niland
Rick Novtny
James Nugent
Jennifer Wolf Nugent
William Seth Null
Taliesin Katherine Nyala
Vasily O
Eric Oakes
Jon Oates
Patrick O'Connor
Jon Oligino
Joanna L. Olin
Timothy Olson
Greg Omasta
Timothy Crocker O'Neill
Brandon Osman
Jerad Ostrowski
Lorri Ostrowski
Angel Oyola
Andrew Page
Jon Palmer
Keegan Park
Daniel Parker
Matthew Parker
James Parsons
Donald Patry
Barb Pepin
Ron Pepin
George Petroff
Michael Philbrook
David Pikul
Mike Pitruzzello
Joshua Polak
Sarah Cohen Polak
Chops Polcari

Matthew Pollard
Jeffery Pollen
Tina Polley
Hans Porschitz
Jerry Pratt
Walter Price
Albert Prokop
Bert Prokop
Scott Proulx
Yvonne Provost
Clifford Wallace Putney
Ngawang Rabga
Dan Raih
Brett Ramsay
Robyn Reed
Bob Regan
Doug Reitmeyer
Eric Remillard
Gloria Reyes
David Rhoads
Julie Evelyn Richardson
Andy Rida
Ron Risdon
Flavio Risech-Ozeguera
Marci Ann Riseman
Rene Robinson
William Rodgers
Dennis Rodrig
Jared Rodrig
Annie G. Rogers
Sigmund J. Roos
Marc Rosenbaum
Karina Eliana Rosenstein
Kenneth Rosenthal
Will Rosenthal
Clement Roy
Jacob Roy
Michael Roy
Robert Roy
Victor Rubio
Eric Phillip Rudnick
Leslie Rudnick
Paula Rudnick

In the job trailer at the R.W. Kern Center.

Abraham Ruiz
Tom Rule
Scott Runey
Samantha
Kim Saal
Aiden Frederick Sagerman
Evan Sagerman
Piper Rosalee Sagerman
Andras Sajo
R. J. Sakai
Carol Salzman
Eduardo Samaniego
Todd Sampson
Ariel Schecter
Bruce Scheible
Robert Schlitter
Walter Schmalenberg
Morwin Schmookler
Schwartzberg Family
William Scott
John Searle
Michael Sears
Jacques Senecal
Troy Senecal
Todd Sessions
Christopher Severance
Daniel Shaw
Debbie Shaw
Gary Sheldon
Jesse Sheldon
Jim Sheldon
Kyle Sheldon
Mike Sheldon
Nick Sheldon
Rick Sheldon
Robin Sheldon
Tina Shen
Patricia N. Shillington
Dennis Shockro
Arlette Sieckmann
Ted Sieckmann
Robert Alexander Sieczkiewicz
Lyle Sienkiewicz

Guillermo Sierra
N. Thomas Sigel
Sean Simmer
Amy Lynn Simpson
Martin Skuse
John R. Slepian
Jeffery Slesinski
Nancy A. Slowe
James Small
Ryan Smarr
Kathleen Smith
Shad Smith
Tabby Smith
Corinne Sodders
Andrew Solem
Matthew Somerville
Joshua Spencer
Anne Spier-Mazor
Mark K. Spiro
Scott Spitzer
Nicole E. Spring
Jeffrey Starratt
Kelly Stasny
Rebecca L. Stein
Charley Stevenson
John Sticklen
Erik Stiles
Wayne Stocker
Kevin Stowell
Lindsay Stromgren
Mary Stuart
Amanda Sturgeon
Ashley Sullivan
Benjamin Swain
Roy Swain
Renee M. Sweeney
Anthony Switzer
Alexander Sylvain
Joe Szuch
Michael Talbot
David Tanguay
Constantin Taraburca
Jeff Tarascio

Jonathan Tauer
Ray Tebo
Mike Tenczar
Brian Tetreault
Carolyn Thayer
James Thomas
Donna J. Thompson
Edgar S. Thompson
Jon Thompson
Laney Thornton
Peter Timothy
Hester Chanler Tittmann
John Tobiason
Diana Tobin
Robert Tobin
Todd Tobin
Elise Kathryn Trelegan
Jeremy Tudryn
Scott Michael Tundermann
Kerry Uhler
Jeffrey Alan Urbina
Carol Louise Varney
Matt Vayda
Ramon Velazquez
Suzanne Velez
Amelia W.
Darlene Wage
Zilong Wang
Alison Warner

David Waskiewicz
Carl H. Weber
Howard Philip Wein
Lenny Weiss
Dan West
Mark Whalen
Rick Whitcomb
Dominique White
Phillip White
Stash White
Jim Wiernasz
Charles Williams, Jr.
Elizabeth Wilson
Peter Witiwiec
Mark Howard Wittow
Jeffrey A. Wolfman
Dylan Woolf
Matthew Worley
Jonathan Wright
Sam Wright
Laurie Wunch
Barnaby Young
Brian Zakizewswki
Juecheng Zhao
Mingda Zhao
Clark Lyman Ziegler
Charles Zilinski
Michaelann Zimmerman
David Ziomek

All Hands Honor Roll: Hitchcock Center For The Environment

A compilation of all those who touched the project in some way, from fundraising, to gifts, to labor, to design, with apologies if your name was overlooked.

Harvey Allen
Justin Allenby
Phil Andrikidis
Reid Atkinson
Aaron Avery
Lynn Badgett
Darin Bajnoci
Daniel Barshak
Phil Bartlett
Mike Bartos
Sam Batchelor
Marcel Beaulieu
Casey Beebe
Penny Beebe
Scott Belanger
Scott Blackwell
Tammy Boutwell
Dan Bradbury
Jim Brassord
Ginny Brewer
Joe Brosseau
Merle Bruno
Margaret Bullitt-Jonas
Robert Burek
Melissa Caldwell
Anne Cann
Vivienne Carey
Mark Carrington
Alex Carson
Brian Casey
Mike Cendrowski
Mike Chambers
Ken Chmura
Casey Clark
Mike Clark

Andy Clogston
Carey Clouse
Roger Cooney
Heather Courchaine
Jaana Cutson
Jaime Davila
Tom Decker
John DeFalco
Steve Dejoy
Karina Delgando
Thomas Devine
Daniel deWit
Phil Deyman
Juan Dominquez
Michael Dover
Addison Duarte
James duBois-Sector
Thomas Duda
David Dunn
Mary Dunn
Nancy Eddy
Valerie Faille
Elizabeth Farnsworth
Pat Flanagan
Lucas Fradette
Mike Frank
Hannah French
Richard Garrison
Kinda Gaudreau
Aiidan Gibbons
Kim Gladding
Ilse Godfrey
Robert Godfrey
Tina Gonzalez
Mike Greancy

Eric Haberman
Kelly Haigh
Charlie Haight
Jeff Hamilton
Caroline Hanna
Tom Harris
Bill Hart
Sierra Hausthor
Dave Healy
Susan Heitker
Marie Hess
Doug Hodgins
Tom Holden
Justine G. Holdsworth
Martha Hoopes
Sam Hughes
Jim Hutto
George Iracheta
Marianne Jakus
Peter Jessop
Eric Johnson
Julie Johnson
Robert Johnson
Shelly Kahan
Doug Kalinowski
Deepta Kamma
Nancy Karella
Colleen Kelley
Bob Kelly
David Knauer
Kristine Koczaiowski
Katie Koerten
Peter Koerten
Paul Korpita
John Kowaleski
Sarah laCour
Joshua LaFlamme
Kate Lamdin
Nick Larochelle
Mark Ledwell
Ann Ledwell
Ron Lefebvre
Chris Leno

Annie Leonard
Ellen Leuchs
Greggory Lewis
Steve Lilly
Jay List
Bridgit Litchfield
Chuck Longsworth
Susan Loring-Wells
Harvey Lussier
Fred Maguire
Ed Mahar
Rob Mahar
Tony Maroulis
Doug Marshall
Jeff Mazur
Micky McKinley
Andrew McNulty
Peter Miccoli
Bob Miklos
Chris Miklos
Joe Miles
Matthew Moynihan
Stephanie Moynihan
Jim Muka
Vinny Muto
Rebecca Neimark
Orin Nisenson
Marty Noblick
Marty Norden
Patrick O'Donnell
Patty O'Donnell
John Olver
Jerad Ostrowski
John Palmer
Phillip Panidis
Anne Perkins
Michael Philbrook
Andy Phillips
David Pikul
Lauren Potter
Scotte Rae
Alison Ray
Keith Raymond

Peter Rayton
Bob Regan
Scott Renney
Dave Richard
Joey Ricker
Chris Riddle
Stan Rosenberg
Geoff Roske
Roy Sabourin
Mary Santiago
Bob Saul
Walter Schmalenberg
Jessica Schultz
Tom Schulz

Michael Schwartz
Evan Scott
Ann Sephton
Lisa Sihvonen-Binder
Marcus Simon
Jim Small
Mike Smith
Eric Smola
Sonya Sofield
Andrew Solem
Bob Stafford
Pamela Stone
Ellen Story
Bill Sweeney

William Telega
Carolyn Thayer
Jeremy Tudryn
Artem Tverdokhlebov
Elicey Tverdokhlebov
Vladimir Tverdokhlebov
Jennifer Unkles
Matt Vayda
Angelo Vigliotto
David Volpe
Ted Watt
Pete Westover
Stash White
Phil White

Michael Wickles
David Wickles
Matt Wilcox
Donna Wiley
Larry Winship
Jonathan Wright
Dan Ziomek

Hitchcock Center for the Environment groundbreaking.

Creating Sustainable Buildings That Renew Our World

Photographs and Illustrations

The author, designer, and publisher are grateful to the following project participants, artists, and photographers for providing an abundance of images.

JOHN AVERILL: pages 54, 60, 68

SAM BATCHELOR: pages 110

ROBERT BENSON: pages 3, 30, 36

BRUNER/COTT: pages 4, 5, 48, 58, 73, 81, 82, 84, 85, 86, 88, 108

MELISSA CALDWELL: page 66

JOHN COURTEMANCHE: page 82

JAN RUBY CRYSTAL: page 46

SARA DRAPER: pages 100, 101

LINDA GAUDREAU: pages 67, 149

KELLY ARD HAIGH: page 42

HAMPSHIRE COLLEGE: pages 10, 11

JASON JEWHURST: pages 37, 145

JENNIFER JOUBERT: pages 26, 27, 73, 114, 123

BILL KERN: pages 29, 60, 61, 74, 77, 84, 135

ANN LEDWELL: pages 47, 72, 79

TOM LUCIA: pages 52, 76, 92, 93, 94

NASA: page 137

CHRISTOPHER NIELSEN: pages 55, 59, 78, 79, 102

MICHAEL SACCA: pages 30, 31, 56

JESSICA SCHULTZ: pages 65, 90, 91,106, 111, 117-121, 125, 138, 151

SHUTTERSTOCK: page 137

ANDREW SOLEM: Pages 68, 69, 70

PETER VANDERWARKER: Pages 49, 106, 116

CARL WEBER: pages 19-25, 40, 41, 74, 97, 108, 113, 130

WIKIMEDIA COMMONS: page 128

JONATHAN A. WRIGHT: pages 21, 32, 34, 35, 44, 48, 50, 52, 57, 63, 64, 69, 71, 72, 74, 76, 77, 80, 85, 89, 94, 95, 96, 97, 105, 108, 109, 112, 119, 122, 126, 127, 131, 132

INTERNATIONAL
LIVING FUTURE
INSTITUTE℠

INTERNATIONAL LIVING FUTURE INSTITUTE

The International Living Future Institute (ILFI) is a hub for visionary programs. ILFI offers global strategies for lasting sustainability, partnering with local communities to create grounded and relevant solutions, including green building and infrastructure solutions on scales ranging from single room renovations to neighborhoods or whole cities. ILFI administers the Living Building Challenge and the Living Community Challenge, the built environment's most rigorous and ambitious performance standards. It is also home to Ecotone Publishing, a unique publishing house dedicated to telling the story of the green building movement's pioneering thinkers and practitioners.

LIVING BUILDING CHALLENGE

The Living Building Challenge is the built environment's most rigorous performance standard. It calls for the creation of building projects at all scales that operate as cleanly, beautifully, and efficiently as nature's architecture. To be certified under the Challenge, projects must meet a series of ambitious performance requirements, including net zero energy, waste, and water, over a minimum of twelve months of continuous occupancy.

ECOTONE PUBLISHING

Founded by green building experts in 2004, Ecotone Publishing is dedicated to meeting the growing demand for authoritative and accessible books on sustainable design, materials selection and building techniques in North America and beyond. Ecotone searches out and documents inspiring projects, visionary people, and innovative trends that are leading the design industry to transformational change toward a healthier planet.

More Books from Ecotone Publishing

Ecotone publications are available online at the Ecotone Bookstore at **living-future.org/bookstore** and at other select retailers.

All proceeds from book sales go to supporting International Living Future Institute advocacy and programming.

THE LIVING BUILDING CHALLENGE SERIES

THIS PAGE:
BUILDING IN BLOOM by Mary Adam Thomas

LIVING BUILDING EDUCATION by Chris Hellstern

OPPOSITE:
GENERATION GREEN by Michael D. Berrisford

DESERT RAIN HOUSE by Juliet Grable

THE GREENEST BUILDING by Mary Adam Thomas

BROCK ENVIRONMENTAL CENTER FOR A LIVING CHESAPEAKE by Juliet Grable

154

GENERATION GREEN
The Making of the
UniverCity Childcare Centre

*LIVING BUILDING
CHALLENGE SERIES*

MICHAEL D. BERRISFORD

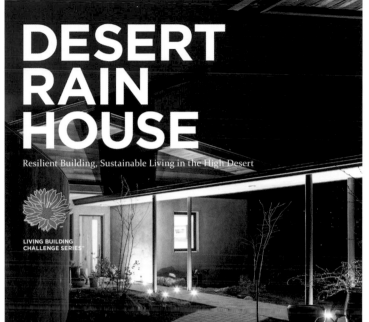

DESERT
RAIN
HOUSE

Resilient Building, Sustainable Living in the High Desert

*LIVING BUILDING
CHALLENGE SERIES*

JULIET GRABLE

THE
GREENEST
BUILDING

How the Bullitt Center
Changes the Urban Landscape

*LIVING BUILDING
CHALLENGE SERIES*

MARY ADAM THOMAS

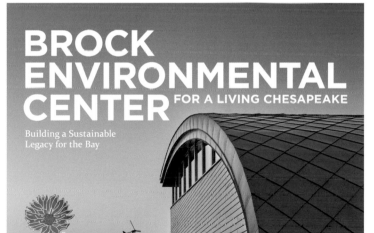

BROCK
ENVIRONMENTAL
CENTER FOR A LIVING CHESAPEAKE

Building a Sustainable
Legacy for the Bay

*LIVING BUILDING
CHALLENGE SERIES*

JULIET GRABLE

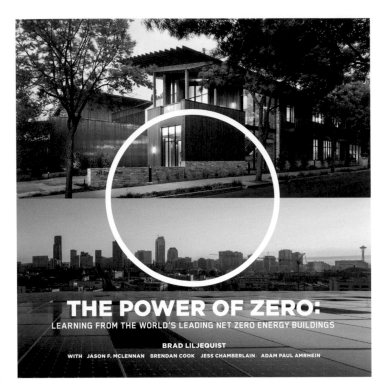

THE POWER OF ZERO:
LEARNING FROM THE WORLD'S LEADING NET ZERO ENERGY BUILDINGS

BRAD LILJEQUIST

WITH   JASON F. MCLENNAN · BRENDAN COOK · JESS CHAMBERLAIN · ADAM PAUL AMRHEIN

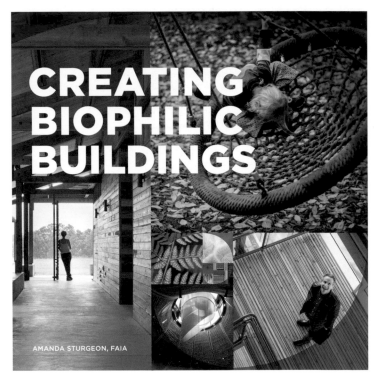

CREATING
BIOPHILIC
BUILDINGS

AMANDA STURGEON, FAIA

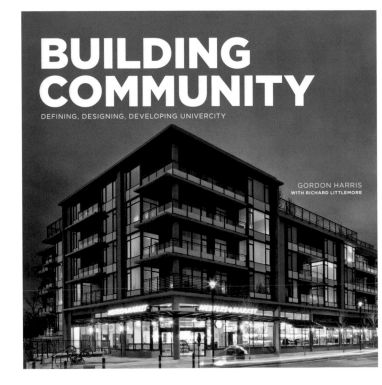

BUILDING
COMMUNITY

DEFINING, DESIGNING, DEVELOPING UNIVERCITY

GORDON HARRIS
WITH RICHARD LITTLEMORE

THE LIVING
BUILDING
CHALLENGE

ROOTS AND RISE OF THE WORLD'S
GREENEST STANDARD

MARY ADAM THOMAS
FOREWORD BY DENIS HAYES

A MANIFESTO IN THE GUISE OF A STANDARD

THIS PAGE:
TRANSFORMATIONAL THOUGHT: RADICAL IDEAS TO REMAKE THE BUILT ENVIRONMENT
by Jason F. McLennan

TRANSFORMATIONAL THOUGHT II: MORE RADICAL IDEAS TO REMAKE THE BUILT ENVIRONMENT
by Jason F. McLennan

ZUGUNRUHE: THE INNER MIGRATION TO PROFOUND ENVIRONMENTAL CHANGE
by Jason F. McLennan

THE PHILOSOPHY OF SUSTAINABLE DESIGN
by Jason F. McLennan

OPPOSITE:
THE POWER OF ZERO: LEARNING FROM THE WORLD'S LEADING NET ZERO ENERGY BUILDINGS
by Brad Liljequist

CREATING BIOPHILIC BUILDINGS
by Amanda Sturgeon, FAIA

BUILDING COMMUNITY: DEFINING, DESIGNING, DEVELOPING UNIVERCITY
by Gordon Harris

THE LIVING BUILDING CHALLENGE: ROOTS AND RISE OF THE WORLD'S GREENEST STANDARD
by Mary Adam Thomas

BUSBY: ARCHITECTURE'S NEW EDGES

PERKINS+WILL   ECOtone

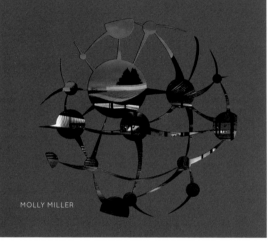

INTÉGRAL

Revolutionary
Engineering

MOLLY MILLER

the
ecological
engineer

Volume Two:
GLUMAC

DAVID R. MACAULAY

integrated
design

MITHŪN

DAVID R. MACAULAY